Amazing Love

FR KEN BARKER MGL

Modotti Press
AN IMPRINT OF CONNOR COURT PUBLISHING

Published in 2012 by Connor Court Publishing Pty Ltd

Copyright © Ken Barker 2012

ALL RIGHTS RESERVED. This book contains material protected under International and Federal Copyright Laws and Treaties. Any unauthorised reprint or use of this material is prohibited. No part of this book may be reproduced or transmitted in any form or by any means, electronic or mechanical, including photocopying, recording, or by any information storage and retrieval system without express written permission from the publisher.

Nihil Obstat
Rev Warwick G. Tonkin BA, DipEd, BTh, MEd
Censor Deputatis

Imprimatur
Most Rev Mark B. Coleridge BA DD, DSS
Archbishop of Brisbane

Connor Court Publishing Pty Ltd
PO Box 1
Ballan VIC 3342
sales@connorcourt.com
www.connorcourt.com

ISBN: 9781921421662 (pbk.)

Cover design by Ian James and cover painting, "Jesus on the Cross", by Br. Mario Venzo SJ (14.2.1900-1.9.1989) from Galarate, Italy.

Printed in Australia

Scripture quotations are from the Revised Standard Version Bible, used with permission.

CONTENTS

Foreword by Archbishop Mark Coleridge   1

Introduction   3

1. God's Plan of Love   11
2. The Human Predicament   19
3. The Word Was Made Flesh   33
4. God in Christ Reconciles   41
5. Transforming Love   53
6. The Father's Heart   67
7. Redeeming Sacrifice   73
8. Deliverance From Evil   85
9. Resurrection: Our Hope   99
10. Jesus Is Lord   109
11. Jesus Heals   117
12. Meaning In Suffering   129
13. Amazing Love   141

Postscript: Redemption Theology   147

Endnotes   153

REFERENCES TO CHURCH DOCUMENTS

CC *Catechism of the Catholic Church*

DV *Dominum et Vivificantem* (Encyclical Pope John Paul II)

GS *Gaudium et Spes* (Church in the Modern world: Vatican II)

LG *Lumen Gentium* (Dogmatic Constitution of the Church: Vatican II)

RH *Redemptor Hominis* (Encyclical Pope John Paul II)

RM *Redemptoris Missio* (Encyclical Pope John Paul II)

RP *Reconciliatio et Paenitentia* (Exhortation Pope John Paul II)

SD *Salvifici Doloris* (Apostolic Letter Pope John Paul II)

FOREWORD

It was in 1979 that Pope John Paul II first used the phrase "new evangelization". This was during his unforgettable first visit to Poland as Pope, and he spent the next twenty-five years of his pontificate unpacking what it means to speak of a new evangelization. Pope Benedict has carried the process further, even to the point of establishing in Rome a new office to promote the new evangelization. Yet there are still people who are unsure what exactly the phrase means. This book of Fr Ken Barker helps to answer that question.

One thing is clear: we need a new surge of Gospel energy in a world where nothing could or can be the same after the twin apocalypse of World Wars I and II. We need a proclamation of the Gospel that is "new in ardour, method and expression", as Pope John Paul put it.

Fr Barker makes it clear that we also need a proclamation that goes back to the basics – by which I mean a new surge of Gospel energy that derives its energy from the encounter with Jesus crucified and risen. Not just Jesus understood as role-model, teacher or miracle-worker, but Jesus risen from the dead, the Son of God and Saviour of the world, the Jesus who is here and now.

Fr Barker also stresses that we need to do more than speak about Jesus or seek to understand him. We need now to *experience* Jesus, his presence and power. That will begin by a proclamation of the kerygma, which we too often take for granted. Insofar as we take that first proclamation for granted, Christianity will seem more and more like a moralism. It will look like a matter of us trying harder and harder to improve and ultimately save ourselves – knowing deep in our heart that we cannot do it. If that is all Christianity is, then people are right to turn away.

Here we have a text that is clear, though never trite. It draws upon the riches of Scripture and Tradition but also includes stories which give it a personal and contemporary touch. It presents in fresh ways the words and images that have come from the past, and it uses anecdotes and examples from the present which illumine in simple and engaging ways.

In the end, Fr Barker shows that a new evangelization is all about opening people to a new experience of the love lavished on us by God in Jesus crucified and risen. It implies not an ideological package nor a political programme, but an overwhelming experience of love. In calling this love "amazing", Fr Barker echoes Pope John Paul II who, in his first Encyclical Letter in 1979, wrote that Christianity is nothing other than an experience of amazement – amazement at what we discover of both God and the human being when we encounter the crucified Lord risen from the dead (*Redemptor Hominis*, 10).

I am confident that this book will be a real help as we set about the great apostolic task that is given to the whole Church now and that we call "the new evangelization".

Archbishop Mark Coleridge

INTRODUCTION

For the word of the cross may be illogical to those who are not on the way to salvation, but those of us who are on the way see it as God's power to save us.
1 Cor 1:18

Now is the time for a fresh proclamation of the gospel. Today, as never before, the Catholic Church has a God-given opportunity for a new evangelization. Blessed John Paul II made an urgent call to the Church, which is still yet to be fully heeded:

> God is opening before the Church the horizons of a humanity more fully prepared for the sowing of the Gospel. I sense that the moment has come to commit all of the Church's energies to a new evangelization and to the mission ad gentes. No believer in Christ, no institution of the Church can avoid this supreme duty: to proclaim Christ to all people. (RM 3)

If ever there was a time when people needed to be rescued from the depths of pain and depression by the revelation of God's love, that time is now. If ever there was a time that the human race needed the light of Christ and the power of his salvation, that time is now. So too, if ever there was a time we needed a revival in dynamic evangelization, rising up with one voice as Church to proclaim Christ, that time is now.

In recent years, through the leadership of the Popes, the Church has been going through a remarkable "evangelical shift"[1]. But like a large ocean liner having to radically change course, this is a lengthy process. Many are seeking to heed the call of John Paul II for a new evangelization[2] marked by new ardor, new methods and new expression. Much effort has gone into using modern technology of communication, developing creative programs, and devising ways to attract people back to their parishes. All this is necessary and very laudable. But there is a more fundamental question. What is *the content* of the message we are seeking to communicate?

Pope John Paul II was insistent that while we need new methods of evangelization we must remain faithful to the content of the gospel, which never changes. If the gospel were to arise from us, and from our situation, it would not be the gospel, but merely a human invention. There would be no salvation in it. Is it possible that some of those who are at the front line of these new efforts to evangelize are not really clear about the message they are meant to be proclaiming? Is it possible that they are not sure of what the basic gospel message is? Is it possible that some may be unwittingly presenting a version of the "gospel" that lacks authenticity? Is it possible that some are not convinced of the redemptive power of the death and resurrection of Jesus Christ? Is it possible that some have not been personally moved in the depth of their hearts by the Cross of Christ, and have not opened their hearts to his saving love? Is it possible that they have not encountered personally the Risen Christ in such a way that they know him as their Lord?

Even if we faithfully teach young people and adults the Church's doctrine and moral law from the Catechism, and introduce them to the sacramental life, this of itself does not guarantee a living personal faith in Jesus Christ as Saviour and Lord. We can fall into the trap of trying to catechize and "sacramentalize" people without first evangelizing them. It is not an "either-or" situation, rather a matter of priority. Which comes first? To catechize people before evangelizing them runs the risk of an intellectual adherence to dogmas with no personal love for the Saviour. To gain sacramental adherence without evangelization runs the risk of formalism and ritualism without a living worship of God rising from a heart truly converted to Jesus. Faith comes from hearing the preaching of the gospel.

Effective evangelization, according to John Paul II, "begins with the clear and emphatic proclamation of the gospel, which is directed to every person. Therefore, it is necessary to awaken again in believers a full relationship with Christ, mankind's only Saviour. Only from a personal relationship with Jesus can an effective evangelization develop."[3] Christianity is not primarily a doctrine, but a person, Jesus Christ. The most important priority is the proclamation of this person and our relationship with him. This is the beginning of all true evangelization. To reverse this order by putting the doctrines and moral obligations before the discovery of a personal encounter with Jesus, would be to "put the cart before the horse."

The situation of the Church in the secularized Western world is not unlike that of the nascent Christian Church described in the Acts of the Apostles. After the outpouring of the Spirit at Pentecost the apostles did not hesitate to boldly proclaim that Jesus is the Lord. They preached a simple message under the power of the Holy Spirit. In the same way as the apostles evangelized the pre-Christian world, we are to evangelize the post-Christian world of our times. The apostles announced what God had done in Jesus Christ through his passion, death and resurrection i.e. the kerygma. This proclamation of the basic gospel message birthed the Church. In our age the same proclamation of the gospel in the power of the Spirit will *re-birth* the Church.

Faith is born from hearing the kerygma, from listening to the proclamation of the gospel. This is what people are waiting for. Their lives are empty, and their hearts are hungry for the Good News of Jesus. In the early Church the content of the apostles' proclamation was simply the work of Jesus of Nazareth. It was summed up in one cry: "Jesus is Lord!" – something that no-one can say "except by the Spirit" (1 Cor 12:3). Whenever, they preached they went to the heart of the gospel, proclaiming two events; the death and resurrection of Jesus. They announced that Jesus of Nazareth had "died for our sins, and was raised for our justification" (1 Cor 15:4; Rom 4:25). Consequently "Jesus is the Lord".

This fundamental gospel proclamation has been likened to a ploughshare, the kind of sword in front of the plough that first breaks the earth and allows the plough to mark out the furrow and turn over the earth.[4] There is much plowing to be done after the first breaking open of the earth; but, without the initial thrust, what follows can be somewhat confused and ineffective. Another image that has been used is a ship's bow. The point of the bow breaks through the water first, and then leaves behind it an ever increasing wake. From the sharp point of the fundamental proclamation of the gospel the body of the preaching and teaching of the Church enlarges itself, until it is truly immense in its depth and width. But it begins with that point which is the kerygma, the basic proclamation of the saving death of Jesus and his Resurrection into glory.

St Paul's letters emphasize the inherent power of the proclamation of the gospel for salvation. He tells the Corinthians that Christ sent him not to preach in terms of philosophy, but to preach the "word of the Cross" which is "God's power to save" (1 Cor 1:17-18). When it is proclaimed with conviction and authority people are brought to repentance and faith. They are confronted with the impossibility of their human condition without Christ. They turn to the source of their salvation, the crucified Lord. They repent and commit their lives to him as Saviour and Lord (1 Cor 1:23-24). Paul had arrived in Corinth after he had tried unsuccessfully to meet the philosophers in Athens on their own terms. He was sharper in his proclamation of the basic gospel:

> During my stay with you, the only knowledge I claimed to have was about Jesus, and only about him as the crucified Christ…there were none of the arguments that belong to philosophy; only a demonstration of the power of the Spirit. (1 Cor 2:1-5)

How did Paul preach the gospel? We get an insight into this from his exhortation to the Galatians, who had been convinced by "Judaisers" from Jerusalem that they should go back to rely on the

Mosaic Law for their salvation. He berates them:

> You foolish Galatians! Who has bewitched you? It was before your eyes that Jesus Christ was publicly exhibited as crucified! ... Did you receive the Spirit by doing the works of the law or by believing what you heard? (Gal 3:1-2)

In his preaching Paul plainly portrayed before their eyes of faith the truth of Jesus' crucifixion. He graphically presented the crucified Christ. However, it was not just a proclamation of Good Friday without Easter Sunday. For Paul, the crucified Christ was the Christ who had died for our sins and was now Risen and glorified, the one whom he met on the road to Damascus. He proclaimed the saving power of the dying and rising of Jesus, and consequently that "Jesus is the Lord". He reminds the Galatians that after hearing the gospel they changed their hearts and made their act of faith in what Jesus had accomplished for them on the Cross and through his resurrection. It was then that they experienced the outpouring of the Holy Spirit. Why would they return to relying on the Law, which has no power to save?

Could it be that some Catholics today are like the Galatians, still too bound by legal prescriptions and works to attain salvation, rather than discovering the amazing love of Christ who has come to save us, and surrendering to his love?

This book aims to expound the basic gospel message, the germinating nucleus of the whole Catholic enterprise. With our strong dogmatic and theological tradition, our immense patrimony of laws and institutions, and our rich liturgical celebrations, we run the risk of losing touch with the primordial nucleus capable of awakening faith. All the renewal stimulated by the Second Vatican Council focused on a rediscovery of the paschal mystery (the death and resurrection of Jesus) and its power in our lives. Yet, strangely enough it seems many are yet somewhat confused about this fundamental core of the faith. Even theologians are struggling to articulate it for the contemporary age.

I am aware of how around the world Catholics are abandoning the mother Church for other Christian groups precisely because they are attracted by a simple and effective announcement of the gospel, which leads them to a personal encounter with Christ and opens them to the power of the Holy Spirit. This phenomenon underlines the need for members of the Church themselves to be evangelized. Pope John Paul II spoke of this impoverished state of some Catholics: "Sometimes even Catholics have lost or never had the chance to experience Christ personally: not Christ as a mere 'paradigm' or 'value', but as the living Lord, 'the way, the truth, and the life'" (Jn 14:6).[5] Thankfully many adult Catholics, especially through the ecclesial movements, have had an opportunity to hear the kerygma, renew their baptism, and consciously choose Christ as their own personal Saviour and Lord, and then commit themselves actively in the life of the Church.

This book, as I have said, is not about how to preach, but about *what* we preach. It is an exploration into the mystery of the redemptive love of God made visible in Jesus Christ. It seeks to explain what Jesus has done for us and why he did it. Its focus is on the power of the Cross and resurrection of Jesus for our salvation. It will necessarily touch on theological controversies, but is not aiming to tackle them, apart from making some options clear when describing what Jesus has done for us. There are some who choose to ignore the Cross of Jesus in their preaching, and it is not unusual for practising Catholics to receive only one homily a year on the Cross, and that on Good Friday. Yet a good homily on the Cross of Jesus, more than any other, can open hearts that have hardened.

First, we will need to look at the mystery of God's love in creating us. Then we will explore how the human race has sinned and separated itself from God. With that background, we will then look at the Incarnation, Death and Resurrection of Jesus, seeking to show how and why we were redeemed. Then we will explore our personal response – repentance and faith. There are further chapters on Healing and Suffering as ways we participate in the redemption. While I give some mention to the outpouring of the Spirit at Pentecost, I have decided to deal more explicitly with the role of the Holy Spirit in a later book, which, God willing, will be the sequel to this volume.

I have occasionally illustrated the various perspectives on the Redemption by true stories of people who have personally experienced the love of God and his saving power. These are testimonies of people who I have met along the way. Only those names which include the surname are true to life. All other names of people whose stories are included here have been changed to protect their confidentiality. I am grateful to those who were willing to share their stories, since this helps to put flesh on the principles I am seeking to present. I have also introduced occasional parables to offer insight at the level of symbolic consciousness, which can be more impactful than an analytical, reflective teaching. For this reason also I have, here and there, called upon the example of the saints.

The book is neither an attempt at preaching, nor an effort at systematic theology. It is probably situated most appropriately as a spiritual reflection. I am hoping it will speak to all Catholics, and to anyone who is honestly seeking Jesus Christ and his significance for us. I hope that it will also serve to stimulate preachers, and give food for reflection for evangelists and all pastors and teachers in the Church. Unfortunately, until recently we have been better at being pastors than being evangelists, better at being shepherds than being fishers. I trust that this little volume will help equip us more for the task ahead. As Pope Benedict said recently, "The key theme of this year and the years ahead is this: how do we proclaim the gospel today? How can faith as a living force become a reality today? ... If faith does not take on a new life, deep conviction and real strength from the encounter with Jesus Christ, then all other reforms will remain ineffective."[6]

1
God's Plan of Love

For it was you who created my being, knit me together in mother's womb. I thank you for the wonder of my being, for the wonders of all your creation.
Ps 139:13-14

Creation

From beginning to end, the history of salvation is the story of God's love for us. His love is infinite and unconditional. Because of his love he seeks union with us. We are his beloved. He seeks to captivate us with his love. For this reason he gave us the beauty of his creation. Out of love he displays for us the beauty of a sunset, the grandeur of mountain ranges, the roar of waves crashing on the seashore. All of creation's beauty speaks of God's immense love for us. Touched by his love, we become grateful for such a bountiful Creator, and want to return his love. St Bonaventure told us God created all things "not to increase his glory, but to show it forth and to communicate it."[7] He has no other reason for creating than his love and his goodness. Thomas Aquinas added, "Creation came into existence when the key of love opened his hand."[8]

The whole of creation gives glory to God. The psalmist articulates this cosmic praise:

> Praise him sun and moon, praise him, shining stars. Praise him, highest heavens ... Praise the Lord from the earth; sea creatures and all oceans; fire and hail, snow and mist, stormy winds.. all mountains and hills, all fruit trees and cedars; beasts, wild and tame, reptiles and birds on the wing ... Let them praise the name of the Lord. (Ps 148:1, 7-10, 13)

All creatures praise him by their very existence. The last words of the Psalter say it all, "Let everything that breathes give praise to the Lord" (Ps 150:6). The whole of creation belongs to God, and reveals his radiant glory.

Human beings are the pinnacle of God's creation. We have the awesome dignity of consciously articulating the praise of the entire creation. Endowed with spiritual faculties of mind and will, we exist to give glory to God; to praise, honour and worship him. God created us out of love to have full life in him. Through this depth of relationship with God, we know him and love him, and we give glory to him. As Irenaeus said, "the glory of God is man fully alive; moreover man's life is the vision of God …"[9]

Creation shares in the goodness of God. In Genesis, after each stage of creation, the author says, "And God saw that it was good …" (Gen 1:10-25). But after the creation of human beings the author says, "And God saw that it was *very* good" (Gen 1:31). This is because God had a purpose for human beings way beyond anything else he had created. God said,

> Let us make man in our own image, in the likeness of ourselves and let them be masters of the fish of the sea, the birds of heaven, all the wild beasts and all the reptiles that crawl upon the earth. (Gen 1:26)

The first thing we notice is that God made each individual in his image and likeness. God defined human beings in terms of our relationship with him. We are made in the image of God; this is fundamental to our being. We are each individually called to participate in the being of God. The second thing we notice is that God says, "Let *us* create man and woman…in *our* image." Here is a hidden reference to the Trinity. God is not only creating Adam and Eve as individuals to be in relationship with him, but also as a couple, who together, especially in sexual union, image the life of the Trinity. This bestows great dignity to the sexual union in marriage, calling this union of self-giving love an icon of the Trinity. It also proclaims that human beings are fundamentally relational, and are meant to be in communion with one another in bonds of love at all levels of our earthly existence. The third thing we notice is that God willed creation to be a gift for us, and he entrusted it to us. We are to be stewards of his creation; co-creators with him, sharing in the on-going work of his creative love. The Psalmist prays with wonder:

> When I see the heavens, the work of your hands, the moon and the stars which you arranged, what is man that you should keep him in mind, mortal man that you care for him? Yet you have made him little less than a god; with glory and honour you crowned him, gave him power over the works of your hand, put all things under his feet. (Ps 8:4-7)

Even though we are stewards of creation, God remains the one and only Lord. While he entrusts us with the care of his creation, no being exists unless God constantly keeps it in existence, and does not let it slip back into nothingness. As stewards we cannot make anything out of nothing. We can only use and transform what we have been given. We are co-workers and collaborators. In reality we are totally and radically dependent on the Creator for everything. If we lose this true order of our relationship with the Creator we lose ourselves.

Of all the creatures on the earth only human beings are able to know and love God. Human beings are "the only creatures on earth that God willed for his own sake" (GS 24, 3). We are called to share in the very life of God. This capacity to participate in the nature of God has bestowed inestimable dignity on each human person. As Catherine of Siena exclaimed:

> O eternal Father, how then did you create this creature? I am greatly overwhelmed by this. In fact, as you show me, I see that you didn't do this for any other reason if not because in your light you were forced to give us being by the fire of your love in spite of all the iniquities we were to commit against you, O Eternal Father!

> It was fire therefore that forced you to do so. O ineffable love, even if in your light you saw all the iniquities your creature was to commit against your infinite goodness, you pretended almost not to see but fixed your eyes on the beauty of your creature whom you, intoxicated with love, loved, and through love you drew her to yourself and formed her in your own image and likeness. You, eternal truth, communicated your truth to me, that it was love that forced you to create her ...[10]

We don't have to go looking elsewhere to find the evidence of God's love for us. We just have to look at ourselves. Each person is living proof of God's love. My being is itself a gift of love. In the light of faith we can know that we exist because we are loved. To be human is to be loved.

Only through the light of the revelation of God's love for us can we truly find our place in the world and know our true identity as human beings. Without this revelation we are impoverished and diminished. Deeply within ourselves we crave for self-worth and a sense of personal dignity, for security and a sense of stability, for significance and a sense of meaning and purpose. Much of contemporary disorientation and identity confusion is simply because we do not know who we are in God. To lose God, especially to lose the knowledge of the love of God, is like being in a boat without an oar or rudder, tossed on the stormy sea, condemned to an aimless and futile existence. We need to know personally that God has created each one in his image and likeness with the purpose of sharing in his nature. We are created to actually share in the eternal love between the Father and the Son. Jesus at the Last Supper prayed to the Father for us, "that the love with which you loved me may be in them, and I may be in them" (Jn 17:26). A child finds personal security when the parents love one another and the child can partake in that love. If this love is breached the child suffers. Similarly we find our security because we partake in the infinite love of the persons in the Trinity. To know this truth anchors us in life and frees us to be our true selves.

God is real and he cares

As a young man Peter took to the party scene, and relationships with women, to try and fulfill a deep longing in his heart to be happy and fulfilled. This desperate search left him feeling empty. In his brokenness, he had a deep desire to be established as someone important in the eyes of others. He desperately wanted to be a success through high achievement. Then people would love him. He turned to sport as a way to establish his identity. Being a competition squash player, he worked hard to attain professional status and make a name for himself. Everything seemed to be going well, and he was on the cusp of success, when the bottom fell out of his life. He was unexpectedly diagnosed with cancer.

After hearing the bad news, his parents arrived at the hospital where he had undergone the tests. They were inconsolable. Peter was still quite cool about it all. The reality had not yet hit him. But while driving home alone, he began to realize what this could mean. There would be no more squash. He would be sick, and maybe he would die. The full weight of his predicament was crashing in upon him. He had to pull over to the side of the road. For the first time in adult life he wept uncontrollably. He was shaking with fear and anger. Peter had heard people talk about God's love. But now he was angrily questioning, "Where is God in all of this? Is he real? Doesn't he care?"

Then at this moment of severe crisis Peter was overwhelmed by a Love he had not experienced before. "I knew it was God; that he is real. And he cares about me!" Peter relates, "It was not a big voice or anything like that. But I now knew everything was OK, no matter what happened." Peter was drawn to the Scriptures. He says, "It seemed that the Bible had been written just for me." In the Scriptures he found amazingly consoling words and the assurance of God's faithfulness. He discovered that "Salvation was not just for the whole world, but something very personal. Jesus died for me. He is now risen and present with me."

After his operation Peter recovered and is now going on with his life. He says there have been many ups and downs, but this personal relationship with the Lord brought a new steadiness to his life. Even though he could not play competitive squash anymore, it didn't matter. His self-worth was no longer dependent on his achievements, nor on what other people think, but was grounded in God's love for him.

God's plan for us

The Genesis account of creation imaginatively reveals God's original plan of love for us. The garden of Eden depicts a familiarity of Adam and Eve with their Creator, who walks with them in the cool of the evening (Gen 3:8). God's intention in creating us was to be intimate with us in a close relationship of love. However, this intimacy was only possible if we retained our true position as creatures before the Creator; that is, in obedience to him, recognizing our utter dependence on Him for everything. As long as Adam and Eve stayed in this intimacy with God they would not have to suffer or die.

God also created us to be in harmony with one another. This is symbolized by the way Adam and Eve share a communion of persons, respecting their individuality, but living in openness and intimacy, being "naked and unashamed" before one another (Gen 2:25). Their relationship of love in one flesh union, the primordial marriage, was one of mutual self-giving love, and was fruitful in bringing forward children. It was free of all self-centredness, manipulation, or domination. They had total respect for one another as individual, unique body-persons. Their union was free of all lust; not using the other for one's own pleasure or gain. There was no grasping in a greedy way for "what I can get." Rather there was the mutual free gift of one to the other. They recognized their equality as unique persons, and they beautifully complemented one another as man and woman. Their love was pure because they offered themselves to one another freely as a gift; and they each received the gift freely as well.

Adam and Eve also had a gift of self-mastery. As unique individual persons they enjoyed an inner harmony of body and soul. There was no experience of inner conflict between the demands of the body and the imperatives of the soul. They did not experience concupiscence (the drive of the flesh) which after the Fall caused division and conflict in the human heart. They were free from any domination of self- gratifying desires, greed or self-glorification. They also enjoyed a harmony with the rest of creation. As stewards of creation their work was productive and fulfilling, as they collaborated with God in perfecting and caring for creation in a responsible way. This idyllic picture of humanity as God intended was to be ruptured when sin entered the world through the disobedience of Adam and Eve.

A work of the Trinity

By the time of St Paul, Christian reflection on creation had gone through a revolutionary development. Now it is proclaimed that all things were made by the Father, in and through the Son and the Holy Spirit. In the Old Testament this concept had already been suggested through the personification of "Wisdom", "Word" and "Spirit".[11] In the Letter to the Colossians it comes to its full flowering:

> He (Christ) is the image of the unseen God and the first-born of all creation, for in him were created all things in heaven and on earth; everything visible and invisible ... all things were created through him and for him. Before anything was created he existed, and he holds all things in unity. (Col 1:15)

This way of looking back on the creation of the world arose from the realization of the universal impact of the redemption that Christ has won for us. Just as he is the end of everything, so is he the beginning. He is the "Alpha and the Omega" (Rev 1:8). All things were created through him, and, in the end, all things will be reconciled through him. The grand plan was that the Father "would bring everything together under Christ as head, everything in heaven and everything on earth" (Eph 1:10). St Ireneaus speaks of the Father creating, using the Son and the Spirit as "his hands":

> There exists but one God.... he is the Father God, the Creator, the author, the giver of order. He made all things by himself, that is, "by his Word and by his Wisdom", "by the Son and the Spirit who, so to speak", are "his hands". (CC 292)

Here we get in touch with the amazing "broad brush" panoramic picture of our creation and redemption. Some Fathers of the Church went so far as to say that the incarnation was already in the foreknowledge of God before the Fall occurred.[12] So it wasn't that God had to swing into Plan B when the original plan failed. It was already in his mind. Here we are in a mystery beyond our comprehension. Creation and salvation have been united in God's loving plan from all eternity. It makes us wonder at the amazing love of God, who created us, even though he was aware that we would rebel against him. In Ephesians, Paul blesses God the Father of our Lord Jesus Christ, who "before the world was made, chose us, chose us in Christ ... determining that we should become his adopted sons (daughters) through Jesus Christ" (Eph 1:4-5).

In drawing attention to this mystery of God's foreknowledge I don't want to diminish in any way the seriousness of the Fall of humanity and its consequences. Nor do I want to suggest that Adam and Eve, and consequently the rest of the human race, are simply pawns in God's chess game, or puppets on a string. When God establishes his eternal plan of 'predestination,' he includes in it each person's free response to his grace (CC 600).

We can only know the beauty and wonder of Christ as mediator in the creation if we have first discovered the height and length, the breadth and the depth of his saving love in redeeming us from the curse of sin. So let us now turn to examine the sinful predicament of humanity.

2
The Human Predicament

From my sins turn away your face and blot out all my guilt. A pure heart create for me, O God. Ps 51: 11-12

What is the problem?

If God's loving plan for the world is for universal harmony and peace it is obvious that something went terribly wrong. Everywhere we witness disorder and unhappiness afflicting men and women. We are not what we would like to be, nor where we would like to be. Wars, terrorism, criminal activity, atrocities of all kinds are daily news items. At the more personal level, family breakdown, relational dislocation, domestic violence, drug dependency, suicide, and so many other social disruptions continue to plague us. We are so often not at peace with ourselves, with others and with the world at large. Even our relationship with nature is ambiguous with the greedy exploitation of natural resources, the misuse of the environment leading to pollution, and disruption to the normal ecological cycle.

Is it possible to sum up the fundamental cause of this predicament? What is the core problem underlying all of the troubles afflicting our human condition? What has gone wrong? The answer is in one word – sin. It is not a popular word today, but if we don't face the reality of sin, we will never find the solution to our problems. There is much that needs to be fixed in today's world, but without the Redeemer, who can fix sin? Without the Saviour we will be left floundering around in our own mess with no way out.

Here we find an initial difficulty of understanding. Our

contemporaries so often will not admit that sin is the problem. This is a dilemma for the Christian preacher. Only in the light of revelation from God can we be really convinced of sin. Jesus promised the apostles at the Last Supper that the Spirit of truth will come "to convict the world concerning sin" by revealing Jesus as the Redeemer (Jn 16:8). Without the Holy Spirit people can remain blind to the truth about sin, and hence about the need for redemption. They see the consequences of sin but can't identify the cause. They will explain the problem away as a developmental flaw, or a psychological weakness, or the result of social conditioning, or a lack of good education, or simply as a mistake. While these may be circumstantial factors that contribute towards sin, if we ignore the reality of sin, we can never be healed.

The preacher may in the initial proclamation touch hearts by opening up the need for emotional healing and for hope in the midst of unbearable suffering. This is a wise way to meet people with God's word where they are immediately hurting. But the preacher will always need to lead people eventually to face the sin of their lives and repent, by renouncing sin and turning to the Saviour. With infinite compassion, Jesus mixed with outcasts and sinners. He did this not only to bring them the comfort of his loving presence, but also to win them back from their sinful ways. He made it clear that it is not those who are well who need the doctor, but the sick. He said, "I have not come to call the righteous, but sinners to repentance" (Lk 5:32). Consequently, Mark tells us that many well known "sinners" were amongst his followers (Mk 2:15).

Blind to the need

The contemporary mind-set, or world-view, is blind to the need for redemption. The secular way of thinking is a type of darkness, something like an eclipse of the sun, which overtakes the mind. A sort of practical atheism takes over. God is seen as irrelevant to the human project. Life is one-dimensional. The world is like a sealed container, without any openings to the transcendent. Peoples' lives are claustrophobic, locked into a hut without windows or doors, and with no way to God.

In this sort of world-view science and technology are seen as the way to salvation. We can do it. We can build a better world ourselves. With our ingenuity we can solve our problems. We can control our destiny without reference to God. There are echoes here of the Tower of Babel story given in Genesis (Gen 11:1-9). This is another version of the Fall of humankind. Arrogantly, humanity tries to build a tower to the heavens, overreaching human limitations. The attempt fails in an irrevocable breakdown in human communication. The people are scattered over the face of the earth and their language is broken up into many different dialects. The author here is using an ancient legend about the origin of diverse languages to make a profound point. The dislocation in our communion with one another has occurred due to human pride and arrogance. The pretensions of science and technology to be able to build a better world without the saving power of God lead to confusion and disarray. From Greek mythology we are reminded of Prometheus who tried to steal the firebrands from the gods for his own sake; a project that proved to have tortuous consequences.

When the legendary passenger ship, the *Titanic*, was about to leave Southampton dock to make its maiden voyage, someone scribbled on this icon of mankind's progress, "Even God could not sink this ship!" Four days into the voyage, the mighty ship hit an iceberg in the night, and began to sink. The damage was irreparable. Many people lost their lives. Maybe this could be an image of our present situation in the world today. People who think they can solve the world's problems by only addressing the issues of psychological and social development, or cultural and political systems, are like passengers on an imaginary *Titanic*, who decide that the best way to deal with the problem is to busy themselves rearranging the deck chairs. Meanwhile there is a gaping hole in the hull! The "gaping hole" in the hull of human affairs is sin. We will sink if it is not dealt with. That is why we needed a Redeemer. Only the Son of God could deal effectively with the radical problem of our sinful humanity.

Original Sin

The first account of original sin in Genesis is the picturesque account of Adam and Eve who were tempted by Satan to mistrust God. After telling the serpent that God had warned them not to eat the tree of knowledge of good and evil, the serpent fed them the lie, "No! You will not die! God knows in fact that on the day you eat it your eyes will be opened and you will be like gods, knowing good and evil"(Gen 3:4). To partake of the tree of good and evil was to try to usurp God's plan. It was a refusal to accept God as God, and a denial that we are creatures dependent on him. The *Catholic Catechism* puts it succinctly, "Man, tempted by the devil, let his trust in his creator die in his heart, and abusing his freedom, disobeyed God's command" (CC 397). It is the act of choosing self over and against God, an act of mistrust, pride and disobedience.

The consequences of this first disobedience are then portrayed poetically in the Genesis story. The dislocation in our relationship with God led to division within ourselves, a rupture in our relationships with one another, and an alienation with the whole of creation. To be against God is to be against ourselves and to be against others. The original harmony was lost. The story in Genesis describes this loss in striking images. When God finds Adam in the Garden, he asks, "Have you been eating of the tree I forbade you to eat?" Adam replies, "It was the woman you put me with me." Accusation, blame, passing off the responsibility to another, are signs of the disruption that has now entered human relationships. Added to this is God's word to Eve, "Your yearning shall be for your husband, yet he will lord it over you"

(Gen 3:16). Whereas originally they enjoyed a mutually respectful relationship of equality, now man will seek to dominate woman – one of the most harmful results of the Fall, which has done so much damage in relationships between men and women.

Inner harmony and peace in the individual person is also lost because of sin. This is depicted by Adam and Eve feeling shame before one another, and hiding with guilt from God (Gen 3:7). The original integration of body and soul is ruptured. Now lust enters the human heart, no longer respecting the other as a person, but desiring to use the other for one's own pleasure and gain. Self-mastery is now lost, and the human being is interiorly wounded by the inherent drive towards sin, which Paul calls "the flesh", and the tradition has called "concupiscence." Also as a result of original sin death makes its entry into human history. The first parents are told they shall now "return to the soil, as you were taken from it. For dust you are and to dust you shall return" (Gen 3:19 cf. Rom 5:12). Humans now have to endure the debilitating reality of death, yet they await the cry of St Paul in the light of the Risen Christ, "Death, where is your sting?" (1 Cor 15:55).

Human beings are now also alienated from the creation; no longer in harmony as stewards of creation, but doomed to work "by the sweat on your brow," and only by much suffering will human beings attain their fulfillment and their welfare (Gen 3:17-19). The creation itself is affected by the Fall of Adam and Eve. Paul says the creation was subject "to its bondage to decay" (Rom 8:21). Now the whole of creation is groaning, longing for its liberation, "From the beginning to now the whole of creation as, we know, has been groaning in one great act of giving birth"; a new state which can only be found in the Redeemer (Rom 8:22).

Genesis is intent on showing us the cumulative effect of sin on the human race. There is an avalanche of sin that follows upon the original sin. Out of envy, Cain murders his brother Abel. Cain's descendants are full of vengeful violence. Lustful practices contribute further towards the inexorable advance of sin that contaminates the human condition. Once called "good" by God, the earth itself is corrupted by the evil actions of human beings (Gen 6:11-13). The whole world needs a cleansing to bring about a new beginning (Gen 9:1-7). Hence the need for the great flood. But after that catastrophe, sin continues with the Tower of Babel, as we described earlier. Sin advances steadily from one generation to the next. This history of sin is made up of many individual choices that coalesce to make humanity more and more alienated from God.

The transmission of Original Sin

The Catholic tradition from the time of Augustine has clearly taught that every human being is born in original sin. This is not due to personal fault. It is simply due to the fact of being born into fallen humanity. It is not a sin we have personally committed, rather it is a state that we contracted through being born into a fallen human race. We are all in solidarity with Adam, and consequently we were all affected by Adam's sin. St Paul makes a parallel between our solidarity with Adam and our solidarity in Christ, the new Adam. Because Christ in his great love has become one of us, we are all now affected for the good by Christ's obedience, which offsets Adam's disobedience. Paul says:

> Just as one man's trespass led to condemnation for all, so one man's act of righteousness leads to justification and life for all. For just as by the one man's disobedience the many were made sinners, so by the one man's obedience the many will be made righteous. (Rom 5:18-19)

Through the corporate unity of the human race all were implicated in Adam's sin. But even more so, through Christ's solidarity with us, we have all been made righteous. Human nature has been severely wounded by sin. We need the healing and elevating grace of the redemption won for us by Jesus. Baptism frees us from Original Sin, but the consequences of Original Sin remain. We still have to suffer, but now not without meaning. I will deal with this in a later chapter. We still have to die, but death also is redeemed by Christ, so that it is no longer a fearful black hole, but the way to fullness of resurrection life in him. We still have to endure the spiritual battle, being hounded by temptations, but Christ's victory gives us the strength and endurance to be conquerors in him. And we still labour under the on-going battle with concupiscence, the inherent inclination towards sin within us, but in Christ we can grow in virtue and holiness.

Sin of the world

In Scripture, sin is often presented as a personalized force that operates against us and seeks to enslave us. In Genesis the Lord says to Cain, "Why are you angry and downcast? If you are well disposed, ought you not lift your head? But if you are ill disposed is not sin at the door like a crouching beast hungering for you, which you must master?" (Gen 4:7). For Paul, sin is a cosmic force of evil that enters human beings when they submit to it. Sin entered the world through Adam, and has exercised dominion over humans and kept them slaves. This slavery is only overcome when we submit ourselves to Christ (Rom 5-8). When we renounce the old ways of darkness, we come through faith and baptism into the light of the community of the redeemed. Paul encourages the Colossians to give thanks to God, the Father, "who has enabled you to share in the inheritance of the saints in the light. He has rescued us from the power of darkness and transferred us into the kingdom of his beloved Son, in whom we have redemption, the forgiveness of sins" (Col 1:12-14).

In John, Jesus gives the disciple a choice between the kingdom of darkness and the kingdom of light, a choice between hatred and falsehood, between love and truth. To choose darkness is to submit oneself to the devil, who is a "murderer from the beginning", "the prince of darkness", "the father of lies". All sinners are "children of the devil" (1 Jn 3:10). On the other hand "God is light. In him there is no darkness … If we live our lives in the light we are in union with one another, and the blood of Jesus, his Son, purifies us from all sin" (1 Jn 1:5-7). John tells us we must make a choice to come out of the "world", meaning the way of thinking, valuing and living which is opposed to the kingdom of light. He says, "the whole world lies under the power of the evil one" (1 Jn 5-19). Conversion will take us out of that contaminated and corrupt environment and place us in the Christian community where there is the joy of the Risen Lord, bringing light and truth.

The Church has always maintained that sin properly speaking refers to the personal attitudes and actions of individuals, since it involves the freedom of each individual person, and not properly of a group or a community. Nevertheless Blessed John Paul II acknowledged the reality of social structures of sin. He said that sin is "the radical cause of all wounds and divisions between people" (RP 4). He then went on to say that the concept of "social sin" recognizes our solidarity with others in the Church, and indeed in the society as a whole. Every individual's sin affects others because of our interconnectedness. Just as we can think of an ascending scale of holiness leading us towards the communion of saints, we can also think of a descending scale of wickedness by which the attitudes and actions of sinners can drag down all the members of the Church, and in some sense the whole society. Just as the holiness of the saints can lift us all towards God, so also can we talk about its sinful counterpart; the sin of the members can have a negative effect on the whole Church, and the sins of individuals can amount to a profound collective oppression in the society. The remedy is not found simply by seeking to change oppressive structures, but by aiming towards conversion of heart. Without genuine individual conversion of heart, changes in the social arena will not hold and cannot be maintained (RP 16).

Personal sin

St Paul proclaims baldly, "all have sinned and fallen short of the glory of God" (Rom 3:23). St John says it just as clearly, "If we say we have no sin we deceive ourselves, and the truth is not in us. If we confess our sins he who is faithful and just will forgive us our sins and cleanse us from all unrighteousness" (1 Jn 1:8-9). In the light of God's love, especially through the action of the Holy Spirit, and by meditating on the passion of Christ, we can have revealed to us the sinfulness of our hearts. Blessed John Paul II expresses it this way:

"Conversion requires convincing of sin…the action of the Spirit of truth in man's inmost being…In this 'convincing concerning sin' we receive a double gift: the gift of the truth of conscience and the gift of the centrality of redemption. The Spirit of truth is the Comforter" (DV 31:2).

St Augustine gives three definitions of sin that complement one another:

> a) Sin is "any deed, word or desire against the eternal law."[13] It is disobedience against the will of God.
>
> b) Sin is "love of oneself even to contempt of God."[14] This is the fundamental selfishness so prevalent in our contemporary narcissistic society.
>
> c) Sin is a "turning away from God and a turning towards creatures."[15] It is a form of idolatry, bowing to the creature, rather than to God. We see this idolatry behind all sorts of addictions – hooked on alcohol, drugs, sex, shopping, or even on people – when we are "bent towards a creature,"[16] rather than worshipping the living God.

The way out of personal sin is by repentance. We need the Spirit to remove the "heart of stone" and replace it with "a new heart and a new spirit" (Ez 36:26). Jeremiah reminds us that "The heart is more devious than any other thing, perverse too: who can pierce its secrets? I the Lord, search to the heart" (Jer 17:10). Jesus laments, "This people honours me with lip-service, while their hearts are far from me" (Mk 7:6). We need a "change of heart"; a complete turn around. Nothing else will suffice.

The sin of our lives can be represented by a tree in a garden with many roots. The roots would represent the deep sinfulness in the heart that needs to be cut out. Maybe the disorder of lust, or greed or gluttony; possibly anger, envy or sloth or vanity. Roots are means by which the tree obtains nourishment and the way the tree stays firmly in place. We need to set the axe to the roots of the tree. As we do, however, we will find that there is a deep tap-root which is not at first obvious as we go about the task, but inevitably becomes the most difficult root to dislodge. This tap root is pride. This is the sin of Adam and Eve in the garden. They were tempted by Satan to be like God "without God, before God and not in accordance with God".[17]

In our personal sin we ratify our complicity in the sin of Adam, and so become personally responsible. Paul describes this fundamental human disorder to which we are all prone, "The wrath of God is revealed from heaven against all the impiety and depravity of men ... they knew God yet they refused to honour him or to thank him" (Rom 1:18-28). This sin of "impiety" is the refusal to accept the fundamental purpose of our existence, which is to give praise, honour and glory to God here on earth and to be with him forever in heaven. Mistrust, pride and disobedience, which began with Adam, can easily control our lives also, and the underlying current of our lives is that we live for the glory of ourselves, rather than for the glory of God.

The way out of slavery to sin is repentance, a decision made under grace to turn from sin and to turn fully toward the Lord Jesus our redeemer. We need to be open and honest about our need for the saving power of Jesus in our lives. It is easy to rationalize sin away: "I am just a victim of circumstances!" or "I just can't help myself" or "It's all their fault anyway!" Our blindness can be sometimes like David. After having arranged for Uriah the Hittite to be killed in order to satisfy his lust for Uriah's wife, he was unable to see his sin. Then Nathan, the prophet, came to David to tell him a story about a rich man in the land who had forcibly taken a poor man's only lamb for himself in order to feed a guest. David was inflamed with anger at this injustice. "As the Lord lives," he said to Nathan, "that man deserves to die." And Nathan said to David, "You are the man!" (2 Sam 12:7). The Holy Spirit will convict us in this way: "You are the one!" While it may be laudable to see the sin of the world and deplore it, the Lord is always challenging us to look at our own hearts first.

From darkness to light

When Phillip finally came away from the Reconciliation room he felt he could dance and sing and praise God all night. His confession to the priest had taken one and a half hours. Under the grace of God, he had humbly poured out the sins of his life in lurid detail. Unfortunately, during his late teens Phillip had managed to chalk up a criminal record, having been arrested for drug possession and being a "public mischief". Plagued with suicidal thoughts he had in his low times been clinging to life by a thread. His life had become out of control and ruled by darkness. Now through the grace of the Sacrament he felt flooded with light, overwhelmed by "the power of God's amazing love," filling him with joy and gratitude. While making his confession the Lord gave him the grace to see in graphic detail the full extent of his transgression, and how loathsome his sins were. But as he confessed with a contrite heart, his heart was flooded with the endless stream of God's mercy and forgiveness, flowing from the Cross of Jesus.

Phillip had been asked to come to the Christian youth summer school by a friend. He had agreed to go, but not with any big expectations. Prior to this, he had already benefitted from six months of weekly scriptural teachings from a renewal community, which had awakened a thirst in him for the love of God. Now through the

Sacrament of Reconciliation he was totally engulfed by the experience of God's love. He felt completely unworthy of this gift of forgiving love. He saw clearly for the first time the ugliness of his sins. But more than this, he had revealed to him the immense mercy of God.

During prayer with others later in the week Phillip was able to visualize bundling up all of the shame and guilt of his sins and giving it over to Jesus, who on the Cross has cancelled the guilt owing to sin, and taken away our shame. He was then able to freely commit himself with all his heart to the One who cared for him unconditionally, regardless of what he had done. Today Phillip continues to live a committed life in the Church, and is full of gratitude to God, who rescued him from power of darkness, and brought him into the Kingdom of light and love.

Phillip's testimony speaks of his shame being washed away in the Sacrament by the cleansing blood of Jesus. So many people walk through life keeping up the good appearances as if everything is fine. But deep inside there is a secret area that is out of control, and they are afraid to let others know about it. A lot of effort goes into keeping the mask in place, trying to avoid others finding out about the disorder. They are terrified of being caught out. But, there is such a relief in finally confessing, and acknowledging our need for the redeeming power of Christ to be able to set us free. There is nothing in our lives that cannot be healed and recreated if we are only willing to be vulnerable and open it up to the Lord, and maybe also to a trusted person who can pray with us. Especially in the Sacrament of Reconciliation we have a precious gift; being able to bare the soul to the priest in confidence, and allow the Lord to take our shame away.

The "First Gospel"

We have looked at how God from the beginning intended us to be in peace with him and others and ourselves, and how humanity's sin frustrated this plan. However, the Genesis message is that God did not abandon us. Rather, he immediately promised salvation. God spoke to the serpent, "I will put enmity between you and the woman, and between your offspring and hers; he will strike your head, and you will strike his heel" (Gen 3:15). We call this the "protoevangelium" or "first gospel," the announcement of the Redeemer; that there would be a battle between the serpent and the Woman, and a descendant of hers would have final victory over Satan. Already there was an anticipation of a "new Adam" who would have victory over the enemy of our human nature. In the Church's tradition the "woman" was often identified as Mary, the "new Eve," who would be born without original sin, and be the one to give birth to the Saviour. Let us now turn to the mystery of the Incarnation.

3
The Word Was Made Flesh

What we have seen with our eyes, what we have looked at and touched with our hands – the Word who is life – this is our subject. 1 Jn 1:1

God's love seeks union with us. He is madly in love with us. It is not a cold, dispassionate love. Rather he is crazy about us. We are the pinnacle of his creation and he will go to any lengths to convince us of his love. But if love is the motive for our redemption, how was it accomplished? Sin had broken our relationship with God. Objectively speaking all people were at enmity with God. Consequently we were suffering alienation from ourselves, from others and from the whole of creation. How was this disorder in the moral and spiritual universe to be repaired? Because we had offended God by our disobedience, the whole intelligible order had been disrupted and dislocated.

Paul calls this state as being under the "wrath of God" (Rom 1:18). He does not mean that God was angry and demanding restitution for his offended honour. Rather, the term "wrath of God" refers to the objective state of the separation of humanity from God because of our sin. It speaks of the total incompatibility between the holiness of God and the rebellion of sin. Within this situation we were left hopelessly lost, unable to attain our true purpose and without the resources to do anything about it. The consequence of sin is eternal death, separation from God forever. How was this seemingly unbridgeable chasm that had opened up between God and human kind to be overcome? The resounding answer is found in the New Testament:

> God loved the world so much that he gave us his only Son, so that everyone who believes in him may not be lost but may have eternal life. For God sent his Son into the world, not to condemn the world, but so that through him the world might be saved. (Jn 3:16-17)

The Incarnation was redemptive in its purpose. Since we were alienated from God and it was impossible for us to change our condition, he took the initiative and, with immense love and humility, took on our human flesh, becoming one of us. He was like us in all things but sin. He clothed himself in frail humanity, bearing with us, and for us, all the consequences of sin – being tempted in every way we are, undergoing physical and mental anguish as we do, and embracing unredeemed death in all of its emptiness and desolation.

The icon of Our Lady of Perpetual Help, and other icons of its kind, demonstrate how Jesus was born to die on the Cross for us. The infant Jesus has just leapt into the arms of his Virgin Mother, losing a sandal in his haste. While holding onto his Mother for protection he is looking up apprehensively to the instruments of the passion. This strong link between the incarnation and the passion, death and resurrection of Jesus is important to keep in mind. The ancient Fathers used to say about the Incarnation, "What has not been assumed has not been redeemed." In other words the Son of God assumed totally our frail human condition, body and soul, so that he could redeem us fully.

Out of immeasurable love for us, Jesus entered into solidarity with us completely. We were one with Adam in the sin of the human race. Now Jesus, the new Adam, representing us, took upon himself the sin of the whole world. He chose to be one with us, under the weight of sinful oppression, so that by the power of his love he could break its strength upon the human soul and set us free. "A second Adam to the fight, and to the rescue came."[18] This Adam/Christ contrast vividly reminds us that we are saved not only by God's power and love brought to us "from the outside." Even more surprisingly we are saved "from *the inside*" by the incarnate Son, who has loved us so much that he has become our brother. The second Adam has come to heal and transform humanity forever.

The Adam/Christ parallel is at the heart of Paul's proclamation of the gospel. He introduces Adam as "a type of the one who was to come" (Rom 5:14). The sin of one man, Adam, through our solidarity with him, dragged the whole human race into slavery, subject to spiritual death. The obedience of one man, Christ, the new Adam, through his solidarity with us, delivered the whole human race, making us right with God and with one another (Rom 5:12-17).

Christ as the new Adam also helps us to see how he came not only to restore humanity from its fallen state, but also the whole of creation. Adam and Eve, representing humanity, had responsibility for the care of creation. The disobedience of Adam, and so the whole of the human race, has caused disorder and disfigurement in the entire order of creation. The transformation needed has cosmic dimensions. This is expressed in the gospels. As Jesus hung on the Cross there was an eerie eclipse of the sun (Mk 15:33). At his death there was an earthquake, "the rocks split" (Mt 27:52). Then on Easter morning again there was a "violent earthquake" (Mt 28:2). The passage of Christ to the Father was an upheaval for all creation. Paul tells us that "the creation was subject to futility" due to the disobedience of Adam; but now, because of Christ, "the creation will be set free from its bondage to decay and will obtain the freedom of the glory of the children of God" (Rom 8:21).

Jesus: the way to be human

So now God has become one of us, and one of us is God. What a wonderful mystery of God's condescension. Paul says of Jesus, "He did not cling to his equality with God, but he emptied himself, taking on the condition of a slave, becoming like we are in all things but sin"

(Phil 2: 6-7). What amazing love, and awesome humility!

Christ is Love that was made flesh. God's love has assumed a human form to be able to love and be loved in a human way. He wept as a child in the crib, and he wept later over the death of his friend Lazarus (Jn 11:35), and he wept over Jerusalem, so much did he long to gather them to himself as a hen gathers her chicks (Lk 13:34; 19:41). Love is his name. And what amazing humility. There have been many gods constructed by the religions of the world. We can think of the ancient Greek gods, the gods of the Romans, the Mesopotamian gods of the biblical times, all the tribal gods of thousands of religious groups. All these gods have admirable attributes, and often terrible qualities, but none of them exhibit humility. The only true God, to the contrary, comes to us in humility, born in a stable not fit for human birth, laid in a manger, which was a feeding trough for animals, and then he died a criminal's death by crucifixion. Through his love and humility he broke the power of hatred and pride which had a stranglehold on humanity.

Human beings cannot live without love. This is the fundamental purpose of our existence. Our lives would not make sense without love. Christ, our Redeemer, comes to reveal us to ourselves. In his humanity we rediscover our greatness. By the very fact that "he assumed our human nature", not by absorbing it into his divinity, but by becoming fully like us in all things but sin, he has "raised us to a dignity beyond compare" (RH 8). He was in total solidarity with us:

> For by his Incarnation, he, the Son of God, in a certain way united himself with each person. He worked with human hands, he thought with a human mind. He acted with a human will, and with a human heart he loved. Born of the Virgin Mary, he has truly been made one of us, like to us in all things except sin. (RH 8)

Through his coming to share in our humanity, we now share in his divinity.

We find our true selves in the love of God, who has created us to belong to him. He loves each individual person uniquely and unconditionally. His love establishes each person with inestimable and unrepeatable dignity. Our value is not in our performance, or our wealth or status, or what people think of us, or any other worldly advantage. Our value is not established by what we do, how we perform, what achievements we may attain. Nor is our worth in what we have in the way of wealth, talents, power or status. Rather our true dignity is founded in who we are as sons and daughters of God. John announces "The Word was made flesh", and "To all who received him, who believed in his name, he gave power to become children of God" (Jn 1:12).

God's love is tangible

As a young man William in his later years of High School was weighed down heavily by the burden of his family's troubles. His father was given to outbursts of destructive rage, which made William fearful for the safety of his mother. His Mum, for her part, suffered from fibromyalgia – a disorder in the muscles which causes widespread pain, anxiety, and stress, and can also affect the mind. The family was under severe financial strain. Consequently, William generously worked afternoon and night shifts after school to help pay the bills. The pressure became too much for him. With an over bearing sense of responsibility for his parents and his little brother, he crumpled under the load. The worst thing was that while he felt obliged to provide for the family, he was not able to be in control of their affairs. He felt helpless and hopeless. An awful fatigue beset him due to the relentless work schedule, and his failing efforts to keep up with the school work. He became depressed.

William recalls the day when his interior crisis reached its peak. He walked slowly and somberly up the track to Crackneck Lookout on the Central coast, close to where the family lived. He had been to this favourite place before to ponder life's questions, while gazing upon the vast ocean beyond the cliff face. But this time his mind was full of dark and disordered thoughts. He knew within himself that one of two things would happen on the mountain that day. Either God would show he was real, or William would have to end it all. He had decided he was "over life", and in his dark confusion was thinking that if he removed himself from the scene, maybe it would lead to something changing for the better for everyone. On reaching the top he made a desperate prayer, "God this is it! You know the two options. I am here. What are you going to do about it?"

As he leaned on the railing, looking out to sea, with a sheer drop below him, he waited. After a while, the wind dropped. All was silent. Then suddenly he was overwhelmed by the powerful presence of God. He heard a voice, which he knew to be God, speaking, "I have chosen you for a purpose; you will be my mouthpiece." He had absolutely no doubt it was God. William recalls that, before this encounter on the mountain, he felt "completely disjointed. Where I wanted to be I thought I could not go." Now he felt a beautiful peace come over him. He was immersed in the immensity of God's love, infinitely more vast than the ocean before him. He felt God's love for him personally, "God actually listened to me, and he answered me. He had been with me in all my troubles, but I did not know it. His love was tangible; I felt it. I knew now that irrespective of the circumstances that were out of my control, all would be well. His love would carry me through."

Ten years later William has grown in the Lord's love. Recently married he and his wife are committed to the Lord and share together in the Church's mission of evangelisation.

The dignity of the human person

St Catherine of Siena, reflecting on the love of God the Creator and Redeemer, makes a passionate prayer to the Trinity:

> Why did you so dignify us? With unimaginable love you looked upon your creatures within your very self, and you fell in love with us. So it was love that made you create us and give us being just so that we might taste your supreme eternal good ... O mad lover! And you have need of your creature? It seems to me, for you act as if you could not live without her, in spite of the fact that you are Life itself, and everything has life from you and nothing can have life without you. Why then are you so mad? Because you have fallen in love with what you have made! You are pleased and delighted over her within yourself, as if you were drunk with desire for her salvation. She runs away from you and you go looking for her. She strays and you draw closer to her: You clothed yourself in our humanity, and nearer that that you could not have come.[19]

In his first encyclical Blessed John Paul II spoke of the gospel as "deep amazement" at the worth and dignity of every human person (RH 8). This dignity was established first through being created in the image and likeness of God, but was lost to a great extent through sin. It has now been restored through the redemption accomplished in the humanity of Jesus. Christ the Redeemer "fully reveals man to himself". In Christ we can find again the inestimable dignity that belongs to our humanity.

People today often make the classic excuse for sinful behavior: "Oh well, I am only human!" However, in reality sin makes us *less than human*. It is dehumanizing. When we look to Christ, fully human, tempted in every way we are, but without sin, we see the true ideal of humanity. To be perfectly human is to be free of sin, and so to be given freely in love for others. By his example Christ not only shows us the holiness we are called to attain, but he also lifts us towards this state "from within". He came to restore us to our original dignity lost by the Fall, but in doing so he brings us into something even greater.

4

God in Christ Reconciles

The life I now live in the flesh I live by faith in the Son of God, who loved me and gave himself for me. Gal 2:20

Solidarity

We have already reflected on the mystery of the Incarnation in the previous chapter. Jesus' entering into solidarity with us expresses his immeasurable love for us. We were in solidarity with Adam in the sin of the human race. Now Jesus, the new Adam, representing us, takes upon himself the sin of the whole world. He chooses to be one with us, under the weight of sinful oppression, so that by the power of his love he could break its strength upon the human soul and set us free.

Reconciliation between humanity and God was accomplished by God himself, not by us. We were helpless to do anything about our desperate lostness and separation from God. We were living as slaves to sin and under the dominion of Satan. Human beings were doomed to a sort of "hell on earth" in their relationships – characterized by anger, envy, lust, hatred, and every type of destructive behavior. But God had mercy on us in our plight. He entered our fallen state and turned it all around. Paul says:

> It is all God's work. It was God who reconciled us to himself through Christ, and gave us the work of handing on this reconciliation. In other words, God in Christ was reconciling the world to himself, not holding men's faults against them and he has entrusted to us the news that they are reconciled. (2 Cor 5:18-19)

Even though Jesus, the Son of God, was the sinless one, he identified himself fully with our unredeemed state. And from that place he made the "yes" to the Father that we were unable to make. This "yes" of the Son of God to the Father had been happening for all eternity within the Trinity. Now the Son, who has become man, one of us, makes the "yes" on our behalf. This brings our redemption.

The Garden

Jesus' loving choice of solidarity with us meant he freely took our place, by suffering for us. As Jesus entered the Garden of Gethsemane, he utters, "My soul is sorrowful to the point of death …" (Mk 14:34). He was beginning to experience already the torment in his soul which was far greater than any physical torture he would have to endure. The sense of the words here suggest a solitary terror coming over his soul, as if he was suspended in a remote corner of the universe, disconnected from all support and consolation. He sweated drops like blood. This describes a possible but rare medical condition when someone experiences an intense and bewildering paroxysm of fear. The gospels show us Jesus' progressive "abandonment" throughout the passion. He is abandoned by his disciples, who are sleeping at the time he most needs them, and then desert him at the time of his arrest. He is abandoned by the crowds who shouted "Crucify him! Crucify him!" But most deeply of all, he experiences being abandoned by his Father. Already in the Garden, Jesus experiences the anguish of being totally alone, and severed from relationship with others. And as he enters into full solidarity with our sin he is cut off from experiencing the Father's consolation.

Jesus is offered the cup of suffering, which is also the "cup of wrath". It symbolizes the physical sufferings to come, but, even more, the sufferings of his soul as he takes upon himself the sin of the world. If a single man had the whole weight of the physical universe bearing down upon him, he would be crushed instantly. In his passion Jesus has weighing upon him the whole weight of the disfigurement of the moral and spiritual universe crushing his soul. Isaiah prophesied, "He was pierced through for our faults, crushed for our sins. On him lies a punishment that brings us peace, and through his wounds we are healed" (Is 53:5).

Pope Benedict XVI says about this moment, "Because he is the Son, he sees with total clarity the whole foul flood of evil, all the power of lies and pride, all the wiles and cruelty of the evil that masks itself in life yet constantly serves to destroy, debase and crush life. Because he is Son, he experiences deeply all the horror, filth, and baseness that he must drink from the 'chalice' prepared for him: the vast power of sin and death. All this he must take into himself, so that it can be disarmed and defeated in him."[20] No wonder Jesus, in his humanity, begs the Father, "If it is possible, take this cup from me!" It seems too much to bear. But he follows this immediately with the words of trust and obedience which will seal our redemption, "But your will, not mine, be done" (Mk 14:36).

In Hebrews there is a beautiful description of Jesus' prayer in the Garden of Gethsemane: "During his life on earth he offered up prayer and entreaty, aloud and in silent tears, to the one who had the power to save him out of death, and he submitted so humbly that his prayer was heard" (Heb 5:7). The author was probably not only thinking of the experience in Gethsemane, but the whole ministry of Jesus, including his passion. It reminds us that rising in the heart of Jesus constantly was a prayer to the Father not only for himself but for all. Pope Benedict comments, "The Letter to the Hebrews views the whole of Jesus' passion – from the Mount of Olives to the last cry from the Cross – as thoroughly permeated by prayer, one long impassioned plea to God for life in the face of the power of death".[21] The Pope sees Jesus in the Garden and in the whole of his passion crying to God on behalf of all human beings, "he holds up to God the anguish of human existence". His prayer was finally answered in resurrection, when Jesus was glorified.

The Garden was a moment of intense struggle. No doubt Satan returned to suggest that it was all going to be a waste of energy. One can almost hear the taunts of the Enemy, "It will all be in vain; they will reject you anyway!" One striking feature in Gibson's passion was when the serpent appeared in the Garden of Gethsemane to tempt Jesus, just like he had appeared in the Garden of Eden. But Jesus, the new Adam, was not going to be seduced. He dramatically crushed the head of the serpent with his sandaled foot. His "no" to Satan was as decisive as his "yes" to the Father.

Abandonment

We are told by Mark that Jesus was nailed to the Cross at the third hour (9am). Then at the sixth hour (12 noon) there was darkness over the earth, until the ninth hour (3pm) when he died (Mk 15:25, 33). The darkness expresses the cosmic dimensions of what was happening. It was probably an eclipse of the sun. But this exterior darkness was nothing compared to the interior darkness of soul into which Jesus was plunged. He willingly entered into his ultimate solidarity with us, embracing the desolation and separation from the Father which had come as a result of mankind's sin. In the depth of this extraordinary dereliction he cried in a loud voice, "Eloi, Eloi, lama sabchthani?" which means, "My God, my God, why have you abandoned me?" (Mk 15:34). He is quoting the first line of Psalm 22, which ends in a song of hope. These words on the lips of Jesus were not a cry of despair. Rather, they represent the anguish of humanity separated from God by sin. On the Cross, in the soul of Jesus, the holiness of God came into collision with the rebelliousness of sin. Jesus experienced in his soul the total incompatibility between the beauty and purity of God and the ugliness of human transgression. Paul says, "God made the sinless one into sin, so that in him we might become the righteousness of God" (2 Cor 5:21).

Yet deeper than this upheaval in the human soul of Jesus was his total union with the Father in the mission of love to which the Father had sent him. Not for a moment did Jesus lose his trust in the Father. Three years beforehand he had risen out of the waters of the Jordan river and known the Spirit come upon him in the form of a dove, and heard the words of the Father, "You are my Son, the Beloved, my favour rests on you." At this moment of extremity on the Cross, these words echoed in the depths of Jesus' soul. He knew he was Son, and his food was always to do the will of the one who sent him.

What does Paul mean when he says, "God made the sinless one into sin..."? There is no question of Jesus identifying himself with the "no" of sin itself. Jesus is always a pure loving "yes" to the Father. The darkness in his soul is not the experience of hell, which is the punishment for those who hate God. While suffering on the Cross in our place, experiencing in his human soul the full consequences of sin, he is still in full union with God.[22] But this does not soften his pain. The opposite is true. Because he is absolutely sinless he suffers more deeply, more intensely, than any sinful person ever could.[23] For Jesus the suffering is so excessively painful because he is totally innocent and undeserving. In the midst of this unthinkable darkness Jesus does not despair, but makes the perfect act of trust in the Father, who he obeys totally unto death. This is our redemption.

Like a rose trampled on the ground

Pam had a position on God which went something like this: "God is not real, but he is good for people who are hurting. People need someone to believe in." Ironically, Pam was hurting badly, but she did not consider God was relevant to *her* life. As a young woman she gravitated to a group which allowed her to experiment with speed, cocaine, marihuana, and to get plastered with alcohol. She thought she had found the acceptance she was so desperately seeking. In the same search she fell into destructive sexual relationships with boys.

There was still an awful emptiness within her heart. She often wanted to cry, but couldn't bring herself to show that level of vulnerability. She had no satisfactory answer to the persistent question, "Why do I have to live today?"

Pam really wanted others, especially her family, to hear the cry in her heart, but she couldn't communicate it to them. She wanted to tell her Mum how much she loved her, but couldn't do it without getting emotional. To remain safe she would say something mean instead. Her outbursts of rage were really a cry "please love me" or "I want you to know I love you." Pam had been abused as a child, leaving deep scars. Her father had not been present to the family due to mental illness. Mum had to be the bread-winner. Now, as she grew into womanhood, Pam fell into a long term abusive relationship with a young man who had recently been released from jail. She fell pregnant, and was counseled that the responsible decision was to have an abortion. The experience left her shattered, deeply lonely, and full of loss and grief, feeling no one could understand her.

Pam's mother had prayed a novena to St Jude, saint of helpless cases, asking for Pam's conversion. Her mother's heartfelt prayers were answered. Not long after the novena Pam left the relationship and returned home. But she was still feeling lost. One evening her sister invited her to a youth group. Her heart was drawn by the spiritual songs, and she allowed the lyrics to move her towards the Lord. From there she came to a week long Summer School for young people. She was blown away by "the brightly shining and happy people." She still felt lost in darkness. Inspired to make a change, she confessed in the Sacrament of Reconciliation to an older priest who was gentle and full of compassion. She recalls, "Until then I had never really experienced love. I felt like I had been crumpled on the ground. And now God had embraced me. He scooped me up into his loving arms. He allowed me to feel loved." A song about the passion of Jesus spoke to her heart: "Crucified, laid behind the stone. You lived to die, rejected and alone, like a rose trampled on the ground, you took the fall, and thought of me, above all."

The Lamb of God

At the beginning of John's gospel the Baptist points his disciples towards Jesus, "Behold, the lamb of God who takes away the sin of the world" (Jn 1:29). Jesus is identified as the Lamb of the new Passover. At the festival of the Passover, which Jesus attended, throngs of pilgrims converged on Jerusalem, and thousands of lambs were sacrificed in the Temple. A portion of the sacrificed lambs would be taken to be eaten in homes during the Passover meal. This sacred meal was a memorial of the liberating events of the Exodus, when God acted to set Israel free from slavery in Egypt. It was the meal that celebrated their deepest identity as a people, and was in hindsight the Old Testament preparation for the Eucharist.

The first Passover meal was eaten in haste under God's instruction and precipitated Israel's flight from Egypt. The Israelites were to take an unblemished lamb without broken bones, kill it, and sprinkle its blood on the door post. They were to cook it and eat it. If they did this their first born would be spared. If not they would die in the night along with all the first born of the Egyptians. The sacrificial lamb died in place of the first born of the Israelite households. They were instructed to commemorate the Passover meal every year. When the children asked what is the meaning of this meal, the father was to explain, "It is the sacrifice of the Lord's Passover, for he passed over the houses of people of Israel in Egypt, when he slew the Egyptians" (Ex 12:26-27).

In John's gospel Jesus dies on the Cross at the same time that the Passover lambs were slaughtered in the Temple, clearly identifying Jesus as the Paschal Lamb (Jn 19: 31). John points out that the soldiers did not have to break the legs of Jesus, because he was already dead; this was to fulfill the Scripture, "None of his bones shall be broken"

(Ps 34:21), an allusion to the prescribed way the paschal lamb of the old covenant was prepared (Ex 12:5). Paul tells us that "our paschal lamb, Christ, has been sacrificed" (1 Cor 5:7). All of this is proclaiming that Jesus was a sacrificial victim on the Cross, the Lamb of God, who by the shedding of his blood has taken our sins away. We will return to explain the full meaning of the sacrifice of Jesus in a later chapter. For now, we want to focus on how the sacrificial Lamb takes our place and bears our sins for us on the Cross.

In Scripture the image of Jesus as the sacrificial paschal Lamb is linked with the servant songs in the prophet Isaiah. This is important to notice, because during his ministry Jesus saw himself as the "suffering servant," giving his life as "a ransom for the many" (Mk 10:45; Mt 12:15-21). In Isaiah we read, "We had all gone astray like sheep, each taking his own way, and God burdened him with the sins of us all" (Is 53:6). The sacrificial Lamb went to the slaughter for us carrying all of our sins within himself. "He was oppressed, and he was afflicted, yet he did not open his mouth; like a lamb that is led to the slaughter, and like a sheep that before its shearers is silent, so he did not open his mouth" (Is 53:7). In First Peter the same idea is highlighted. We had all gone astray, but "He himself bore our sins in his body on the Cross, so that free from sins, we might live for righteousness, by his wounds you have been healed" (1 Pet 2:24). In order to cleanse us of our sins the Lamb of God first was laden with our sin on the Cross. "He was wounded for our faults, crushed for our iniquities: upon him was the punishment that made us whole, and by his bruises we are healed" (Is 53:5).

In order to redeem us, the Son of God himself went into the depth of our sin-spawned humanity. Innocent though he was, he "bore our sins" for us. On his way to Calvary he fell often under the physical weight of the Cross, but interiorly he was crushed even more by the weight of our sins. He experienced in himself the dreadful desolation and abandonment of all the sin of humanity. Totally forsaken, plunged into a spiritual darkness deeper than any mystic has ever experienced, he kept his heart turned toward the Father in loving obedience. From that spiritual nadir of emptiness, and annihilation, he made the act of trust in the Father that we were unable to make. Whereas we had been disobedient, and warranted the condemnation due to sin, he made the perfect act of obedience which reconciled us to the Father, "Father, into your hands I commend my spirit" (Lk 23:46). This is the sacrifice of the Lamb, slain for our sake, who now has made us right with God and hence capable of being right within ourselves and with one another.

Stories of redemption

Parables can help illustrate this wonderful mystery. There was a farmer whose property had been devastated by a bush-fire. Afterwards, as he was walking around surveying the damage, his eyes fell on a strange black lump on the ground. Nonchalantly he kicked it. And out came six little chickens! When the fire had gone through, the mother hen had instinctively thrown herself over her chickens in an act of self-oblation. She died. They ran free. This is what Jesus has done for us; not by instinct, but by his own choice in love. He has allowed himself to be immolated on the Cross that we may go free! Amazing love!

A little boy had suffered a type of leukemia, but had a surprising recovery. But now his sister was diagnosed with the same disease. The doctors considered that her best chance was to have a blood transfusion from her brother. Since his blood had developed the anti-bodies necessary to combat the disease they were confident the transfusion would bring new life to his sister. The doctor explained the situation to her little brother, and asked the boy if he would be willing to give his blood for his sister. He hesitated a moment before taking a deep breath, saying, "Yes, I will do it for my sister." As the transfusion progressed, the boy was in the bed next to his sister, and was smiling at her. Then he looked up at the doctor and asked with a trembling voice, "When do I start to die?" He had misunderstood the doctor. He thought he was going to give *all* his blood for his sister; that he was going to die for her! Self-sacrificing love! But Jesus *has* given all his blood for our sake. The death of Jesus is an act of perfect love.[24]

In 2007 two US soldiers, Ross and Ian, who were best friends, were on patrol in a Humvee in the streets of Bagdad. Suddenly a live hand grenade was flung into the truck. Ross immediately threw himself over the grenade, taking the full brunt of the explosion and was killed instantly. His selfless sacrifice saved the lives of the other three men in the truck. Ian saw Ross' face as the grenade detonated. The gruesome memory is always with him. But Ian is full of gratitude. He had been hit by shrapnel in many places on his body. But he knew that Ross had saved his life. "I know I should have died that day" he says, "but he gave me my life and he gave me my wife and kids back … how can I thank him enough? I will not waste the gift that has been given to me." Jesus has given himself completely for us, dying on the Cross, so we may live. This is love beyond all telling. How can we thank him enough? We must not waste the precious gift that we have received.[25]

A sign of victory

In the Auschwitz concentration camp in 1941 a prisoner had escaped from block 14. The prisoners from that block were punished by having to stand in the searing sun all day long. In the evening the commander informed them that ten of them would be condemned to death in the starvation bunker. He randomly chose each man with the point of his finger. One of them cried, "Goodbye, my dear wife; goodbye my dear children, already orphans of your father!" Suddenly a prisoner stepped out of the ranks, and walked calmly to the commander. Stunned, the commander asked, "What does this Polish pig want?" The prisoner said, "I am a Polish Catholic priest; I want to take his place because he has a wife and children." The substitution was accepted. Nothing like this had ever been seen before in Auschwitz. Fr Maximilian Kolbe's self-sacrifice was a light in the darkness, a sign that love conquers evil.[26]

He died imitating his Saviour, who said, "Greater love has no man than this, that a man lay down his life for his friends" (Jn 15:13). At the beatification in 1971 Pope Paul VI said "Maximilian Kolbe fulfilled this maxim of redeeming love."[27] At his canonization in 1982 Pope John Paul II said, "This was a victory won over all systematic contempt and hate for man and for what is divine in man – a victory like that won by the Lord Jesus Christ on Calvary. The Church accepts this sign of victory – won through the power of Christ's redemption – with reverence and gratitude."[28] The sacrifice of Maximilian Kolbe, freely offering himself to die by taking the place of another, provides for us a window into the mystery of the Cross of Jesus. On the Cross, Jesus took our place, bearing the consequences of our sin upon himself. Paul reminds us, "The love of Christ urges us on, because we are convinced that one has died for all … And he died for all, so that those who live might live no longer for themselves, but for him who died and was raised for them" (2 Cor 5:14).

The man for whom Maximilian Kolbe made his substitutionary sacrifice was present at the beatification. Reflecting on the incident he said, "At that moment it was hard for me to realize the immensity of the impression that took hold of me. I, the condemned, was to live on and someone else willingly and voluntarily offered his life for me. Was this a dream or reality?"[29] Maybe that question should be our own as we ponder Jesus crucified. Jesus took our place and died for us on Calvary. Have we let the reality dawn on us; have we allowed the magnitude of his sacrifice affect us, and change us? If we do, we will never be the same again.

A Trinitarian event

The whole mystery of the Cross and what has been accomplished for us is a tremendous story of God's amazing love for us. It proclaims the

Father's love, who does not spare his only Son, but gives him up for us all (Jn 3:16; Rom 8:32). It also proclaims the love of the Incarnate Son, who loves us "to the end" (Jn 13:1). The Son was not forced to undergo his passion. He says, "For this reason the Father loves me, because I lay down my life in order to take it up again. No one takes it from me, I lay it down of my own accord, and I have power to take it up again. I have received this command from my Father" (Jn 10:17-18). Thomas Aquinas, commenting on this text, says that Christ freely chose to move towards his passion, and the Father infused into his soul the love and the courage whereby to do it.[30] It is beautiful to realize that the Father did not give over his Son to suffering and death for any other reason than for love of us. And what the Father asked of the Son was nothing else than to love us unto death.

The abandonment of Jesus on the Cross manifests a twofold love. Firstly, there is the love of God the Father letting go of the Son, giving him over into absolute poverty, obedience and self-abandonment, experiencing the darkness of the "divine wrath". Secondly, there is the love of God the Son, who out of gratuitous mercy identifies himself with us, entering into solidarity with us in the horrible pit of sin, and through this act of total trust and obedience accomplishes the will of the Father (Heb 10:7).

Behind this love of the Father and the Son towards humanity is the eternal mutual love of the Father and Son for one another, who is the Holy Spirit. The Holy Spirit of love is symbolized in the gospel accounts of the death of Jesus by the life-giving waters flowing from the side of Christ, and also by the final expiring of Jesus, when he "breathed his last" (Lk 23:46). The love from both the Father and the Son is brought home to us by the activity of the Holy Spirit poured upon us. The Spirit poured into our hearts enlightens us of the truth of God's love, awakens in us a heart of adoration of this tremendous Lover, and draws us into the new way of life won for us by his love.

5
Transforming Love

He loves us and has washed away our sins with his blood Rev 1:1.

In the previous chapter we unveiled the dark abandonment of Jesus on the Cross. Now we move the focus to the one reason why he hung there for us; amazing Love. John of the Cross, who himself was deeply in touch with the reality of Christ's abandonment, also knew the motive in the heart of God, "I looked upon your Cross, O Lord, and I saw there the song of your love."

As Jesus hung on the Cross, the divine love in his human heart was poured out for us all. Gazing upon our crucified Saviour, we realize he is passionately in love with us, and will go to any lengths to win us by his love. We are touched by his love, and inspired to love others. John tells us, "This has taught us love – that he gave up his life for us; and we, too, ought to give up our lives for our brothers" (1 Jn 3:16). But his love on the Cross is more than an ordinary exemplary death. His way of loving overwhelms us and changes us. It is a love that moves us by its beauty and grandeur, and like an irresistible magnetic force draws us into union with him. This is a love that generates more love, and brings energy to our tired hearts. This is a persuasive love, which awakens in us deep gratitude, and redefines the way we see the world, the way we relate with others, and the way we appreciate ourselves. This is a redeeming love that transforms our hearts by its powerful effect upon us.

I have come to bring fire

During his journey towards Jerusalem, Jesus cried out, "I have come to bring fire to the earth and how I wish it were blazing already. There is a baptism I must undergo and how greatly I am constrained until it is accomplished" (Lk 12:49). Burning in the heart of Jesus was a consuming fire of love, the fire of the Spirit, which had been "given to him without reserve" (Jn 3:33). This fire compelled him forward toward his "baptism" of suffering for our sake. The word "baptism" means immersion. He was to be immersed into suffering and death for the salvation of all. Nothing was going to stop him. Earlier in Luke's gospel we are told, "When the days drew near for him to be taken up, he set his face like flint to go to Jerusalem" (Lk 9:51). What was drawing him forward to ultimate collision with the religious authorities? What was propelling him towards a humiliating death by crucifixion at the hands of the Romans? It was the power of love.

I have translated what Jesus experienced in his heart as "greatly constrained". Sometimes it is translated as "greatly distressed", or similar sentiments. Whatever the translation, in his heart Jesus was on fire with a love that must sacrifice, a love which must be expressed by self-giving unto death. We can gain further insight by looking at another place in the New Testament where the same Greek word is used. Paul exclaims to the Corinthians, "The love of Christ constrains us (urges us, overwhelms us, compels us) because we are convinced that one has died for all.. and he died for all, so that those who live might live no longer for themselves" (2 Cor 5:14). Just as Jesus was fired by love to go to his passion, to die for all, so we now find ourselves captured by this same love, and our hearts cannot but be moved. We are won over by love. Our hard hearts are melted, and we freely respond with all we have to our blessed Saviour. And we no longer want to live for ourselves, but to live for others, in the power of his love.

The pierced side of Christ

"God is love" (1 Jn 4:8). This sums up everything that needs to be said. As God is in his being, so he is in his operations. The starting point and centre-piece of any understanding of the redemption won for us by Jesus is found in the heart of Jesus opened up for us on the Cross. In John's gospel we are told that the soldier pierced the side of Christ with a lance, from which flowed blood and water (Jn 19:37). This had been predicted by Jesus earlier when on the last day of the festival he had cried out, "Let anyone who is thirsty come to me, and let the one who believes in me drink. As Scripture says, from his breast shall flow fountains of living water." John tells us, "He was speaking of the Spirit which those who believed in him were to receive; for there was no Spirit yet because Jesus had not yet been glorified" (Jn 7:17-19).

The living water that flowed from the breast of Christ depicted the outpouring of the Spirit, bringing new life. The blood that flowed speaks of his merciful love, given for us until the last drop was shed. "Having loved his own who were in the world, he loved them to the end" (Jn 13:1). John quotes the text from Zechariah, "They will look upon the one whom they have pierced" (Zech 12:10). As we dwell upon the pierced side of Christ we are drawn into a "heart to heart" love for our Saviour. Pope Benedict XVI returns often to the centrality of the pierced heart of Christ for proclaiming the good news of God's redeeming love:

> Adoring contemplation of the side pierced by a lance makes us sensitive to God's salvific will. It makes us able to place our trust in his salvific and merciful love and at the same time strengthens our desire to participate in his work of salvation, becoming his instruments. The gifts received from the open side, from which 'blood and water' poured (Jn 19:34), lead to our lives becoming a source from which 'flow fountains of living water' (Jn 7:38) for others too.[31]

As we gaze upon him whom we have pierced by our sins, we find ourselves moved deeply by his holy wounds, and especially by his heart opened for us. Medical science can corroborate the flow of blood and water from the physical heart of Jesus. But this is not the main point. The biological heart is a symbol of a deeper reality. In biblical understanding, the "heart" is the innermost centre of the human being, from which emerges all our thoughts, desires, decisions and actions. The heart of Jesus, God-man, expresses the decision of his human will, inspired by the Father's love, given to the Father for our sake, and given for us in love. His heart is broken open in passionate sacrificial love for every human being.

The heart of God

The theme of God's loving heart is well attested to in the Old Testament revelation. In Jeremiah we read of his covenantal attitude, "I have loved you with an everlasting love, and I am constant in my affection for you" (Jer 31:3). In Isaiah we hear, "You are precious in my sight, because you are honoured and I love you" (Is 3:4). In the Song of Songs the bridegroom is overwhelmed by the beauty of the bride, "you have ravished my heart" (Song 4:9), and later, "set me as a seal on your heart for love is as strong as death" (Song 8:16). All of the passion of a lover is intended to be present in our relationship with God.

Hosea's canticle of the love of God is an even more compelling witness. He depicts God as a doting Father who lifts up his infant against his cheek, and takes him forward with leading strings of love (Hos 11:4). God madly loves his chosen people, yet he is struggling within himself, because they have rebelled. He should punish them. But he relents, "My heart recoils within me, my compassion grows warm and tender" (Hos 11:8). God's heart struggles between the demands of justice and the graciousness of mercy. Mercy wins over justice. His merciful love conquers him. This upheaval in the heart of God found in Hosea leads us to the Cross. Jesus, the Son of God, takes our place on the Cross. The pierced heart of the crucified Son fulfills the prophecy of the heart of God which "overthrows its righteousness by mercy and by that very action remains righteous."[32]

The forgiving Father

In the New Testament this gospel of mercy is proclaimed exquisitely in Jesus' parable of the prodigal son, which could be called more aptly the parable of the forgiving father (Lk 15:11-24). It is all about the heart of God, expressed through the attitude of the Father to his wayward son. Jesus wanted to show us what the Father is like. This is why Jesus came; to reveal the Father to us. "No one has ever seen God, it is the only Son, who is nearest to the Father's heart, who has made him known" (Jn 1:18). The parable finds its ultimate enactment when Jesus hung on the Cross for us, displaying the Father's mercy.

In the story, when the son decides to return to the Father after squandering all his money on loose living, the Father has already been waiting, yearning for his son's return with all his heart. When he sees the son coming in the distance, he runs to his son, with complete disregard for his own dignity, and throws his arms around his son and kisses him tenderly. He does not ask any probing or embarrassing questions. There is no interrogation at all.

The offence the son committed against the father was great, and would have been felt very deeply. In the Eastern cultural context, in which the parable was set, the son's demand for half of his inheritance was tantamount to saying to his father, "I wish you were dead". Then leaving for a foreign land was a heartless rejection of the home into which he was born and nurtured, and a cutting loose from all the traditions handed down from one generation to the next. When we understand the radical nature of the offence that had been made by the son, we can see even more clearly the unconditional love of the Father. God's mercy has no bounds. The father is not worried about the dishevelled appearance of the son or his reeking smell from living among the pigs. He comes right into the mess of his son's distress and embraces him, kissing him tenderly.

There is probably no better description of what happened on the Cross for us than what is depicted in this parable. If the offence against God is to be measured by the dignity of the person offended, then it was infinite. Yet God chose in his infinite love not to hold our faults against us. He did not demand out of justice that a penalty be paid to make up for the offence. Unlike the gods of the pagans, he does not need to be placated by offering sacrifices to amend for their offences. Rather he willingly stretched out his arms in love for us, and died for us. What amazing love!

Give me your wounded heart

John Pridmore was a gangster in the East End of London. His life was caught up in drug deals, protection rackets, organized crime of all kinds, often involving malicious violence. He had everything money could buy – the penthouse flat, BMW, thousands of dollars weekly to spend as he wanted. Yet in his heart there was a gnawing emptiness which he chose to ignore. He tried to fill the void with heavy drinking, dope, cocaine, and promiscuous relationships.

At the age of ten, John's parents divorced. He says, he made an unconscious decision not to love again. "If you don't love you don't get hurt". At the age of thirteen he began stealing, and at age fifteen he was put in a detention centre. His abusive behavior turned to anger when at age nineteen he was imprisoned in solitary confinement for 23 hours. He came out of this more angry than ever, deciding, "What you want out of life, you have to take". He turned to vicious crime to get what he felt he needed from life, but underneath it was mainly a search for love and respect.

A turning point came when at a West End club, which John partly owned, he hit a man with a knuckle duster. When the man fell to the floor, John was afraid he had killed him. He says the only thought he had was, "I might get ten years for this". Driving home that night John was in shock. "What have I become? That I would kill someone and not even care?" The slow progression into evil had deadened his soul. He says, "I was dead, but didn't know I was dead."

Now the voice of conscience was afflicting his soul. For the first time in his life he knew God was real. But it was a terrifying moment, because he realized that he had shut himself out from God. He felt inside himself the horror of his plight. He cried out for another chance. Immediately he felt lifted up. And he made his first prayer, "Up to now I have just taken from you my God – now I want to give!" He said he felt a "buzz" come over him, much better than any feeling from all the drugs he had experienced. He felt the touch of the Spirit of love.

John went to tell his mother about what had happened. She was overjoyed since she had been praying for him every day of her life. His step father gave him a Bible. He had never read the Bible before in his life. Opening it randomly, his eyes fell on the story of the prodigal son. It bowled him over. He says he knew the young man in the story was him. "Everything I had taken from God I had wasted." Like the young man he knew he was starving, not for food, but for love. "I had spent my life trying to impress others. Now I knew the Father's love for me." John knew that the Father had never stopped searching for him even when he was buried under the rubble of his sins.

At a retreat John heard the priest preaching on the topic, "Give me your wounded heart." The priest explained that "every sin we commit is like a wound on our heart." John relates, "As I was gazing at the crucifix I knew why Jesus died on the Cross. The darkest sins I ever committed he carried in his heart on the Cross." John experienced Jesus saying to him, "John, I loved you so much I would go through this again just for you." John was overwhelmed that someone would love him so much. He went to the sacrament of Confession. It took an hour; but when the priest laid his hands on John's head he knew that it was the hands of Jesus, absolving him. "My sin killed me. Confession brought me back to life." After having lived a life of bitterness and hatred, so often given to unprovoked violence, John says, "The greatest gift given to me is to be able to love." He now has dedicated his life to bringing the love of Jesus to others.

Rich in mercy

Paul proclaims, "What proves that God loves us is that Christ died for us while we were still sinners" (Rom 5:6-8). He is not talking about a proof like you might give as evidence in court, nor like you might do to solve a mathematical problem, or to prove a scientific hypothesis. Rather this is a proof which captivates the heart. "The heart has reasons that reason knows not."[33] We become convinced of God's supreme initiative in redeeming us. By his Spirit of love within our hearts, we are overwhelmed by what he has done for us. We were at enmity with God because of our sin, but that was no deterrent to him at all. In fact the opposite was true. Jesus says, "The Son of man came to seek out and save the lost." It was a sheer act of mercy. We did not earn his love, or do anything to attract him to come, or merit his coming in any way. As John puts it, "This is the love I mean, not our love for God, but God's love for us when he sent his Son to be the sacrifice that takes our sins away"(1 Jn 4:10). Paul underlines the gratuitous nature of our redemption when he reminds the Ephesians how they were all previously governed by the passions of the flesh, following worldly desires like everyone else. "But God," he says "who is rich in mercy, out of great love with which he loved us even when we were dead through our trespasses, made us alive together with Christ … For by grace you have been saved through faith, and this is not your own doing; it is the gift of God" (Eph 2:3-9).

Forgiveness: breaking the cycle of violence

On the Cross Jesus was dealt the ultimate slap in the face. He graciously turned the other cheek. When he was being nailed to the

Cross he did not rise up and smite the soldiers who were inflicting totally unjust and physically horrendous pain upon him. Instead at that very moment he cried out, "Father, forgive them, for they know not what they do" (Lk 23:34). This heart of forgiveness has breathed life into the world, giving us new hope that we are not doomed to an eternal cycle of hatred and violence. No moral evil need have the final victory any more. From the greatest moral evil ever committed, the rejection and murder of God's Son, God's grace abounded all the more, and brought the greatest of all goods, our redemption. Now, if we are prepared to draw our strength from the Cross of Jesus, the creative power of forgiveness is always available. Even in the direst circumstances of injustice, we can find in our heart the grace to forgive.[34]

On the Cross Jesus entered fully into solidarity with us in the deepest wounds of our human condition. Being one with us he turned hatred into love, evil into goodness, slavery into freedom. Enduring Roman crucifixion, the most humiliating condemnation and agonizing execution of that time, he transformed the Cross into a permanent sign of the enduring merciful love of God. Through amazing love he has broken definitively the cycle of hatred and violence that is so destructive for humanity. Anyone who opens their heart to Christ on the Cross, no matter what injustice they have experienced, will be given the power to forgive. Standing at the foot of the Cross we are touched by the mercy of God, and can allow the precious blood of Jesus, shed for each of us, to soften our hearts and empower us to forgive and to embrace one another from the heart.

When Nelson Mandela came to power in South Africa he finally put an end to the racist apartheid policy and initiated a Truth and Reconciliation Commission. Rather than have a Nuremberg style court to condemn the oppressors of the apartheid regime, the Commission, under the leadership of Archbishop Desmond Tutu, chose to take a path towards reconciliation. If oppressors faced their accusers and fully confessed their crime before the Commission they would not be prosecuted for that crime.

A young policeman named van de Broek, together with other officers, had shot an eighteen year old boy and burned the body to destroy the evidence.[35] He also had later returned to the same house and seized the boy's father. The wife was forced to watch as policemen bound her husband on a pile of wood, poured petrol over him, and set him on fire. Now van de Broek was before the Commission admitting to his horrendous crime. After he had pleaded guilty and asked forgiveness, the crowded courtroom became hushed. The atmosphere was tense. What would happen? The elderly widow who had lost both her son and her husband was given a chance to speak. "What do you want from Mr van de Broek?" the judge asked. She replied she wanted the policeman to go to the place where her husband had been burned and to gather up the dust so she could give him a decent burial. Weeping, van de Broek agreed.

Then she added, "Mr van de Broek took my family away from me, and I still have a lot of love to give." She said she wanted the shamed policeman to come to the ghetto and spend a day with her every two weeks so she can be a mother for him. Finally she declared, "I would like Mr van de Broek to know that he is forgiven by God, and that I forgive him, too. I would like to embrace him so he can know my forgiveness is real". As the old woman made her way to the dock to embrace her enemy people in the courtroom began to sing "Amazing Grace". But van de Broek neither heard the hymn being sung, nor was he able to return the embrace. He had fainted, overcome by grace and mercy.

Eyes of mercy

Jesus was crucified with two criminals on either side of him (Lk 23:39-43). One had a hardened heart and joined in the mockery and abuse, "Are you not the Christ? Save yourself and us as well." But the other criminal rebuked this man, proclaiming Jesus' innocence, "we are paying for what we did. But this man has done nothing wrong." This criminal whom we have come to call the "good thief," was undoubtedly guilty of heinous crime; but he was touched deeply by Jesus. Maybe he was caught by the merciful eyes of Jesus turned towards him; the same eyes of mercy which opened Zacchaeus' heart, the same compassionate gaze that led Peter to weep bitterly after his denial. Held by that gaze of mercy, his heart melted. He opened his heart to the saving grace of the crucified Christ. Jesus' promise was to be fulfilled for him, "This day you will be with me in Paradise." How amazing is the love of Christ! At the very moment of excruciating agony, when his whole body was wracked with unbearable pain, rather than think of himself he was intent upon the salvation of this man. Paul says, "Christ did not think of himself" (Rom 15:3). He did not indulge his own feelings. He did not please himself. There is no move for self-preservation in the heart of Jesus on the Cross, no turning inward with self-pity. His heart was opened in love for the world. His self-giving love calls us out of our futile self-preservation, and by handing ourselves over to him we discover the fullness of love which alone will sustain us.

"I thirst"

Our reflection on the love of Jesus crucified becomes even more poignant when we realize that his gaze of mercy was on each one of us, and still is upon each one of us now. At one point he cried out, "I thirst!" In the terrible agony of crucifixion the body became parched through dehydration. But John recalls these words because of their deeper significance. They speak of his thirst for every man and woman, his thirst for our souls, his thirst for union with us, the very purpose of his dying for us.

Earlier in the time of his ministry we are told that his heart was wrenched as he looked out over the crowd because they were "harassed and dejected, like sheep without a shepherd" (Mt 9:36). This deep compassion that rose in the human heart of Jesus was not some generic observation of the crowds. Rather it was his deep heartfelt concern for each unique, individual person in those crowds, his concern for the salvation of every individual. This is his thirst for relationship with each one of us. There has never been a human person come into the world for whom Christ does not thirst. This is the heart of the Good Shepherd who leaves the ninety nine and goes out after the lost (Lk 15:4-7); the Good Shepherd who lays down his life for his sheep (Jn 10:11). Jesus held each one of us in his heart as he hung on the Cross. Even though it was our sins that put him on the Cross, it was his love for each one of us that held him there.

A witness of love

The initial divine inspiration given to Mother Teresa, which motivated all she did, was the revelation of Jesus' thirst, and a deep longing to satiate this thirst. She put the words "I thirst" in all the chapels of the Missionaries of Charity. She saw her vocation, and that of her sisters, to be a "carrier of God's love – We carry on our body and soul the love of an infinite thirsty God – and we ... will satiate that burning thirst..."[36] Some, she said, will do this by untold suffering, others by a labour of love, but always in union with the Cross of Jesus. Towards the end of her life she said, "God is in love with us and keeps giving Himself to the world – through you – through me – May you continue to be the sunshine of His love to your people and thus may your life be something truly beautiful to God."[37] To the degree that we radiate the love of God given in Jesus will our lives be truly beautiful.

Maybe no figure in this age has stirred us to love as has Mother Teresa; challenging us to follow Jesus without counting the cost, to give all for Jesus, in response to his giving all for us. As a young sister she promised Jesus she would never refuse him anything he asked of her. And at the end of her journey she was deeply grateful, that, by the grace of God, she had kept the promise. She simply wanted to be "the spouse of Jesus on the Cross, alone, naked, bleeding, suffering,"[38] fully given in love for others. Her definition of holiness was simply, embracing the Cross of Jesus by "doing the will of God with a smile".

In his Lenten message in 1993, Pope John Paul II, no doubt influenced by his friend Mother Teresa, asked the Church to listen to the voice of Jesus, "who, tired and thirsty, says to the Samaritan woman at Jacob's well: 'Give me a drink'" (Jn 4:7). The Pope urged us, "Look upon Jesus nailed to the Cross, dying, and listen to his faint voice: 'I thirst' (Jn 19:28). Today, Christ repeats his request and relives the torment of his Passion in the poorest of our brothers and sisters." This message of the Pope filled Mother Teresa with great joy.[39] She began to be more open about the underlying purpose of her whole spiritual journey – to satiate the thirst of Jesus, who is suffering in the poor, longing to be met and loved. This is what had drawn her at the beginning to meet her Beloved in the "distressing disguise of the poor".

I once heard Mother Teresa tell the story of one of her young sisters who was struggling to experience Jesus in the poor and abandoned. Mother told her to look carefully in the morning at how gently and lovingly the priest touches the Body of Christ in the Eucharist, and then go out and do the same when she was with the dying. The sister came back at the end of the day very excited. She had picked up a man in the street who had sores all over him, and brought him to the House of Compassion. As she washed him and cleansed his wounds she knew she was loving Jesus in his suffering, satiating the thirst of Jesus to be loved in the poorest of the poor. Mother Teresa also told us to use the "five finger test" at the end of each day of our lives: think back over the day gone past, and all the encounters and interactions with others. Then hear Jesus say the five words, one for each finger: "You did it to me" (Mt 25:40). At the end of our lives we will be examined by our love.

6

The Father's Heart

See what love the Father has given us, that we should be called children of God; and that is what we are. 1 Jn 3:1

Unfortunately there was a mistaken idea in some Christian traditions that God was so offended by the sin of mankind that his anger had to be placated. In taking our place on the Cross, Jesus became the object of God's fury. On Calvary God in justice was punishing mankind for the offence of sin. Jesus took our place and bore that punishment. God was unsatisfied until he had exhausted his vindictiveness on the innocent man Jesus. This distorted interpretation of the Cross was called the "penal substitution" theory.[40]

The problem with the various versions of this "penal" theory is the false idea of God which it conveys. The prevailing image of God in this theory is the opposite of the merciful Father depicted in the parable of the prodigal son. It does not depict the Father who Jesus came to reveal. The true God is summed up in the three words: "God is Love" (1Jn 4:8). The "penal" approach to redemption imagines that God began to rage against humanity, and then changed to love after his anger was appeased by the sacrifice of Jesus. It fails to present the "tender mercy of the heart of our God" (Lk 1:78).

Having then discounted the "penal" approach as an aberration, a further question presents itself. If the Father was not angry and vindictive towards Jesus then was he passive and unengaged as Jesus suffered? Was the father involved, or was he disinterested? This is a vital question for moderns because the issue of human suffering is so much on our hearts. Well might we ask, "Does God care?"

Early in Christian tradition a heresy arose that shaped our thinking on this issue for centuries. It was called "patripassianism", which simply means the suffering of the Father.[41] But the heresy claimed that, just as the Son suffered his horrible physical passion, so did the Father. This was a way of saying there was only one person in God. In reaction to this heresy, in order to defend the doctrine of the Trinity, the theme of the suffering Father was no longer acceptable. It was maintained that the passion was *willed* by the Father and the Son, but suffered only by the Son. In addition, Greek philosophy tended to define God as "impassible," unable to suffer. Because God is unchangeable, immutable, then it seemed logical that he was impassible. But this philosophical position seemed to declare that God is indifferent to the suffering world. Such a position from the logic of philosophy does not sit easily with the revelation in Scripture, and conflicts with the "logic" of the Cross.

Thankfully, in the present era there is a rediscovery of the suffering of the Father. Blessed John Paul II points out how Sacred Scripture "speaks to us of a Father who feels compassion for man, as though sharing his pain. In a word, this inscrutable and indescribable *fatherly* 'pain' will bring about above all the wonderful economy of redemptive love in Jesus Christ, so that ...love can reveal itself in the history of man as stronger than sin." The Pope goes on to say, "in the humanity of Jesus the Redeemer, the *suffering of* God is concretized" (DV 39). We now have the freedom to say that the Father participated in the Son's passion, but the Son remained a distinct person. Only the Son suffered the passion; but the Father *suffered with* him. We speak of the Father's *com-passion*, a "suffering with" the Son. This is more in keeping with the biblical idea of God's suffering with his people, as opposed to the Greek philosophical idea of an impassible God.

Paul says, "Since God did not spare his own Son, but gave him up for us all, we may be certain after such a gift that he will not refuse anything he can give" (Rom 8:32). Here we find the revelation of the heart of the Father in the passion and death of Jesus. The Old Testament prefigurement is found in the story of Abraham going up Mount Moriah with Isaac his only son carrying the wood for the sacrifice (Gen 22:1-19). Abraham was obeying God's command to sacrifice his son Isaac. The heart of Abraham is broken as he goes ahead to give over his only son. As they make the journey, Isaac breaks the silence, and speaks to Abraham, "Father," he said. "Yes, my son," he replied. "Look, here are the fire and the wood, but where is the lamb for the burnt offering?" Abraham answered, "My son, God himself will provide the lamb for the burnt offering." Just imagine the heart of Abraham being pierced as Isaac addresses him as "Father". Maybe this can give us an insight into how God the Father "felt", how he suffered, as he willingly gave over his only Son to be sacrificed for us. Abraham on Mount Moriah was given a reprieve by God. On Calvary, out of love for his Son, and for all humanity, God the Father denied himself that option, but then he wonderfully raised his Son from the dead for our justification.

A loving collaboration

The Father and the Son collaborated in the passion and death of Jesus. At the moment when Jesus felt the greatest abandonment and separation from God that any human being has ever felt, was also the moment when he and the Father were at their deepest intimacy. Possibly we can gain some understanding of this from the experience of the "dark night of the soul" of the mystics, as they are drawn into full union with God. We then need to multiply it infinitely in intensity. It was a blessed collaboration in love.

It was the knowledge of the Father's love that gave Jesus the inner strength and trust to pass through the darkness of his passion retaining his confidence in his ultimate vindication by the Father. In his human consciousness, I suggest, Jesus never forgot for a moment the wonderful experience in the Jordan river after his Baptism, when he was overwhelmed by the Spirit, and heard the words from the Father, "You are my Son, the Beloved, my favour rests on you" (Lk 3:21-22). These words contain the inner secret of Jesus. Throughout his entire journey here on earth it was this intimacy with the Father which defined him most.

Jesus knew himself as Son, "nearest to the Father's heart", with the mission to reveal the Father, and to do the Father's will. His journey unto death was in union with the Father, and indeed his death was his "going to the Father" (Jn 14:28). His passion was his hour of glorification. In John's version of the struggle in his soul Jesus cries out, "My soul is troubled. What shall I say? Father, save me from this hour? But it was for this very reason that I have come to this hour. Father, glorify your name" (Jn 12:27-28). And the Father did glorify his name by raising him from the dead. The whole story of the passion, death and resurrection of Jesus is one of a faithful Father who is determined to bring about our salvation.

The Father never gives up on us

There is a touching story from the Armenian earthquake in 1989 which killed 30,000 people in less than four minutes.[42] A father had taken his son to school every day, and in the evening he was there to bring his son home. He had promised his son, "I will always be there for you. I'll never desert you." When the earthquake struck, in the midst of all the chaos and destruction, the father rushed to the son's school. He found the school had been reduced to rubble. Parents were all there wailing in despair. No one could have survived this devastation. The father ran to the back of the building where his son's class-room was. He began to dig with his bare hands. People tried to stop him "It's too late!" "Go home, there's nothing you can do!" But he kept digging. The police and the fire chief tried to stop him. They insisted it was a futile exercise. Others came to help for a while. But after 24 hours they gave up. But the father kept going, his hands cut and bruised, but his love for his son drove him on. Then after 36 hours he pulled back a large boulder, and heard his son's voice. The father shouted, "Armand!" Back came the words, "Papa! Papa!" Half the kids were still alive. And Armand was heard to say to the other kids, "I told you my Father would save me. He promised me he would always be there for me!"

God, our Father, never gives up on us. He has kept his promise that he will be there for us. He has saved us from the rubble of our sins. On Easter morning He rolled back the stone. With the rolling back of that stone came eternal life, and true and lasting freedom in Christ. And our heavenly Father is still about rolling away stones. Our Father comes to us and with loving determination digs into the rubble of our lives, uncovering the sin which keeps us entombed. He is about removing the stone of despair, the rock of shame, or the boulder that keeps us in bondage. Our Father was so faithful that he raised Jesus from the dead, and, in Christ, he raises us also, bringing forgiveness of our sins and a Spirit-filled life.

7

Redeeming Sacrifice

But as it is, he has appeared once for all at the end of the age to remove sin by the sacrifice of himself. Heb 9:26

Sacrifice is a key concept for the appreciation of the mystery of the redemption. Paul says of himself, "The life I now live in the body I live in faith; faith in the Son of God who loved me and gave himself up for me" (Gal 2:20). Jesus showed his immense love by offering himself as a perfect sacrifice to the Father on our behalf. We will first focus on the sacrifice of Jesus on the Cross as his obedience to the Father unto death. Then we will look at the sacrifice of Jesus as his self-giving love for us.

Sacrifice as obedience

From the outset we must grasp that the New Testament authors, reflecting the practice of the early Church, decisively abandoned the Temple sacrifices of the Mosaic Law. So much so that when the Temple was destroyed in 70AD it had no impact upon Christian worship, which had long since distanced itself from Temple sacrificial worship. The book of Hebrews announces that the "once for all" sacrifice of Jesus Christ is radically new. It is superior to the animal sacrifices of the Temple and surpasses them. Referring almost scornfully to the priests and sacrifices of the Temple, the author of Hebrews compares them with the unique and unrepeatable sacrifice of Christ: "All the priests stand at their duties every day, offering over and over again the same sacrifices which are quite incapable of taking sins away. He on the other hand has offered one single sacrifice for sins … By virtue of this one single offering, he has achieved the eternal perfection of all whom he is sanctifying" (Heb 10:11).

Hebrews presents the sacrifice of Jesus as a supreme act of worship of the Father, but not associated with the Temple cult. In his passion Jesus' offering engaged his whole body. But, unlike the sacrifices of old, his sacrifice was primarily an interior gift of his self to the Father. It was first and foremost an act of obedience to the Father's will, offered on our behalf (Heb 10:7-9). And while his self-offering to the Father climaxed on the Cross, this was, in fact, the story of his whole life here on earth. He was priest of a different kind. He was "completely like his brothers so that he could be compassionate and trustworthy…able to atone for human sins" (Heb 2:17-18). In solidarity with us, his whole purpose was to do the Father's will. "My food is to do the will of the one who sent me" (Jn 4:34) and again, "my aim is not to do my own will, but the will of the one who sent me" (Jn 5:30). In the Garden of Gethsemane he offered himself, "Your will not mine be done," and on the Cross he finally surrendered his whole being, body and soul, to the Father, "Into your hands I commend my Spirit." He was both the priest and the victim, and his sacrificial offering was his will given to the Father on our behalf, which was expressed outwardly by his bodily suffering and death.

"Behold your Mother!"[43]

"Standing near the cross of Jesus was his mother" (Jn 19:25). Every fibre of her being would have been shaken by what she had seen during the passion; and now what she was enduring at the foot of the Cross. Mary was there due to flesh and blood affection, and she wept at the loss of her son. But in God's plan she was there also because of her commitment to share totally in the redemptive sacrifice of Jesus. She is the first disciple, united with him in his suffering, yielding to the Father's will, allowing the sword promised by Simeon's prophecy to pierce her soul (Lk 2:35). As St Bernard said, the wounds that afflicted the body of Jesus were experienced by Mary in her soul. She was the first to partake in the sacrifice of Christ; and will forever be the model of all those who are called to enter into this mystery of redemptive suffering.

On seeing his mother beside the cross, Jesus could well have remembered the idyllic time of Nazareth, and the moment that, at her prompting, his ministry began at Cana. Maybe he recalled the moment of Joseph's death, and of his own separation from her as his ministry absorbed his being; the separation which was her lot in recent years, a separation which was to increase. For her part Mary could have been letting her mind turn back to all those times when "she held these things in her heart" (cf. Lk:19, 51). Now more than ever she understood the connection of these earlier events with the cross. Sorrow and faith were united in her heart. At a certain point she became aware that in the midst of his agony, Jesus was speaking to her.

"When Jesus saw his mother, and the disciple whom he loved standing near, he said to his mother, 'Woman, behold your son!'" (Jn 19:26). It was an act of tenderness. The love of a son for his mother, not wanting her to remain alone. But it was more than this. It was a gesture of the Redeemer of the world, bestowing on Mary, as 'woman', the role of mother of all disciples. At that moment, she was consecrated by her Son as "Mother of the Church." In God's eternal plan Mary has been one with Jesus at the centre of the history of redemption. She has been one with him in his sacrifice to the Father; her will has been one with his perfect offering. Now Jesus goes beyond involving Mary in his offering to the Father. He also makes her one with him in the gift of himself to humanity. With a gesture of supreme detachment, Jesus gave her to us, his last and precious gift to humanity, that of his mother for the Church and to the world. She is now mother for us "in the order of grace" (LG 61). Just as Mary had played a maternal role in the life of Jesus as he grew up in Nazareth, now Jesus wants his disciples to enjoy this same maternal nurture and protection.

Jesus then turned to the Beloved disciple saying, "Behold, your mother!" (Jn 19:27). Jesus asks all of his disciples to treat her as our Mother. The disciples are invited to love Mary as their own Mother. It is as if Jesus is saying, "Love her as I loved her." We are told that John took Mary into his own home. On the one hand, it was a practical gesture to care for a widowed mother who had lost her only son. But more than that, it was symbolic of all disciples of Jesus who now make room for Mary in their lives. She is the beautiful gift of the crucified Christ to every disciple. As we are drawn into sharing in the sacrifice of Jesus, through allowing ourselves to be broken and given on the Cross with him, we have our Blessed Mother as our example, our guide and our help.

Mercy not sacrifice

It is important to understand that the sacrifice of Jesus, and our participation in it, is not in any way an attempt to placate or to appease an angry God. Unfortunately at one stage in the Christian tradition it was common to define sacrifice in this way. By the time of Thomas Aquinas this notion was in vogue. While Thomas' presentation was well nuanced, his definition still contained this mistaken idea: "In the proper meaning of the term one calls sacrifice that which is done to render God due honour with a view to placating him."[44] Contemporary scholars rightly point out that this concept is foreign to the New Testament perspective on the sacrifice of Jesus. According to the Scriptures it was not human beings who went to God with the gifts or virtues for the sacrifice; it was God who provided the means for the sacrifice to take place. The primary initiative is with God, not with us.[45]

We can note here that the Old Testament already had a strong polemic led by the prophets against sacrifices of rams, goats, and bulls that were not true worship from the heart. The psalmist prays,

"You do not ask for sacrifices and offerings, but an open ear. You do not ask for holocausts and victim. Instead here I am" (Ps 40:6-8; cf. Heb 10:5-7). Quoting the prophet Hosea, Jesus challenges the current thinking about sacrifices, "I desire mercy, not sacrifice" (Mt 9:13). Again the penitential psalmist prays, "For in sacrifice you take no delight, burnt offering from me you would spurn, my sacrifice a contrite spirit. A humbled contrite heart you will not spurn" (Ps 51:16-17). So the sacrifice of Jesus is an act of obedience and humility.

Sacrifice is what God does, rather than what we do. We are not focusing on what humanity needed to do in order to please God. Rather, we are full of gratitude for what God has done for us. This perspective helps us from slipping back into a way of thinking akin to the Temple sacrifices of old, or even worse into a sort of unholy alliance with pagan religious rituals.

The mercy seat

Let us look at a fundamental text on redemption, which is at the hub of Paul's message to the Romans. Speaking of Christ, Paul says we are all "justified by his grace as a gift, through the redemption that is in Christ Jesus, whom God put forward as a sacrifice of atonement by his blood, effective through faith" (Rom 3:24-25). This term "atonement" is sometimes translated as "expiation". The Greek word is "hilasterion", which is a translation of the Hebrew "kapporet", meaning "mercy seat". In the Old Testament the mercy seat was the golden cover on the Ark of the Covenant in the Holy of Holies. On the Day of Atonement, or "Yom Kippur", the High Priest went into the Holy of Holies and sprinkled the "mercy seat" with the blood of a bull which had been killed as a sin offering. This blood was understood to wash away the stain of the sins committed by the people in the previous year. Now Paul is proclaiming that Jesus is the one and final "mercy seat."

The Old Testament thinking was that the blood of the victim

mysteriously contains all the sins of the people.[46] When it touches the "mercy seat" it is touching the Divinity. Thus it is cleansed. In the process, the people represented by the blood are also purified through this contact with God. So when Paul designates Jesus as the new definitive "mercy seat" he means that Jesus radically surpasses the effectiveness of the old one in bringing purification. In his self-offering on the Cross, Jesus brings all the sin of the world deep within the love of God, and wipes it away. In the old dispensation, the blood of animals by touching a holy object was seen as effecting reconciliation between God and humanity. However, the sacrifices of old were never sufficient to purify us of our sins. Now with Jesus, the new "mercy seat," we are cleansed totally and in a way that does not need to be repeated again. How is this so?

In the passion, as we have seen, all the filth of the world is carried willingly in the soul of Jesus. It is brought into contact with the infinitely pure one, the Son of God in union with the Father. In the soul of Jesus this brings great upheaval and suffering. But because he is the Son of God, the holiness of God, under the power of his love, wipes out the sin. On the Cross, Jesus the Son, is deeply united with the Father. In his heart there is infinite goodness and love. Yet at the same time the totality of the sin of the world weighs upon him. He carries it within him. Which will be the most powerful? Goodness or wickedness? Certainly Jesus experiences within his human soul sin's resistance to love, and the agony of knowing the Father's total rejection of sin. But he himself is Goodness and Love. As the sin of humanity is brought into contact with the infinite goodness and love in the heart of Christ, love conquers hatred, goodness conquers evil, forgiveness conquers violence.

The drama of our redemption happens within the soul of Christ on the Cross, and more accurately within God himself. We don't subscribe to a theory of redemption which has God demanding punishment, and the need of humanity to satisfy this demand by a bloody sacrifice. Rather we proclaim that God himself is the locus of reconciliation. Jesus, the Son of God, is the "mercy seat" – he takes the consequences of our sin on himself and eliminates it by his love. He drinks the "cup" of horrible human degradation, so that it may be cleansed of all corruption by his love. Through this loving sacrifice humanity can be restored to right relationship with God, with one another and with the entire creation.

Sacrifice as self-giving love

Even though Jesus suffered immensely, the suffering itself does not constitute sacrifice. It could have been an act of masochism. What makes it sacrifice is that he suffered *with such great love*. This opens up another dimension of the meaning of sacrifice. Jesus identified himself with the suffering servant songs of Isaiah (Mt 8:17). His sacrifice was not only an act of obedience to the Father, but in and through this gift of self, it was also a self-giving sacrifice for us. When teaching the apostles about what it means to be a servant, Jesus says, "For the Son of Man himself did not come to be served but to serve and to give his life as a ransom for the many" (Mk 10:45). This reminds us of Isaiah's fourth servant song, "By his sufferings shall my servant justify many, taking their faults on himself" (Is 53:11).

The whole of Jesus' ministry and passion was an act of self-giving love, an act of humble service, which he symbolized at the Last Supper by taking the place of a slave and washing the feet of his apostles (Jn 13:1-16). His words of institution at the Last Supper express eloquently the truth of his whole mission, "This is my body, given for you" and, "This is the cup of my blood poured out for you". He was totally given in love for us, completely poured out as a sacrifice for us. When he broke the bread it spoke already of his body broken on the Cross for us, and even more so of his will broken for us before the Father. By sharing the broken bread, he was inviting his disciples to join him in being broken for others, not preferring themselves, but wanting to do the Fathers will, and ready to be expended in sacrificial service of others. When he offered the cup it was to invite his disciples into his suffering, to enter deeply into his sacrificial love. To drink of the cup was to be prepared to join him in his sacrifice to the Father, and also in pouring out their lives for others.

Speaking about his "hour" of glorification, the imminence of his passion and death, Jesus says in John's gospel:

> Very truly, I tell you. Unless a grain of wheat falls into the earth and dies, it remains just single grain; but if it dies, it bears much fruit. Those who love their life lose it, and those who hate their life in this world will keep it for eternal life. Whoever serves me must follow me, and where I am, there will my servant be also. (Jn 12:23-25)

Jesus refers to his death as being broken open in love for others; just as a grain of wheat is burst open in the ground and dies, so that new life can come forward. He is clearly inviting his followers into imitation of him through dying to self for the sake of others.

Can you drink the cup?

When Oscar Romero was appointed Archbishop of San Salvador in 1977, he was not expected to challenge the status quo. The wealthy land-owners held oppressive power over the poor, and it was in the self-interest of the political elite to maintain this system of inequality and injustice. Six days after his appointment Romero was shocked when the National Guard opened fire on a crowd of ten thousand people gathered to protest against fraudulent elections. Three weeks later one of his priests, who had worked tirelessly to help his parishioners gain human rights from the land-owners, was shot dead, together with two companions. These events brought Romero to his knees. In the movie entitled *Romero*[47] he is depicted as kneeling at the place of the murder, struggling inside himself, knowing that the "cup" is being offered to him. He cries out to the

Lord, "I can't," and a voice from heaven says, "You must!" Then offering his life, he utters softly, "I am yours!" From that moment Archbishop Romero began to speak courageously on behalf of his oppressed people. He never spoke to incite violence. He simply proclaimed the gospel, knowing that he was putting his life at great risk.

His death came suddenly in March 1980. He was shot through the heart by an assassin as he finished the homily at a Mass for the anniversary of a friend's mother. He had just read the gospel from John, given above, "Unless a grain of wheat falls to the ground and dies ...". His final words were recorded:

> This Holy Mass, this Eucharist, is an act of faith. With Christian faith we know that at this moment the wheaten host is changed into the body of the Lord, who offered himself for the world's redemption, and in this chalice the wine is transformed into the blood that was the price of our salvation. May this body immolated and this blood sacrificed for humanity nourish us also, so that we may give our body and blood to suffering and to pain – like Christ, not for self, but to teach justice and peace to our people ...[48]

And then the shot rang out. The video takes artistic license depicting the Archbishop shot at the moment he was holding up the chalice after the consecration. He fell to the ground and his blood was mingled with the blood of Jesus which flowed from the chalice. This is a gripping symbol of the meaning of Eucharistic sacrifice, which *is* the sacrifice of Jesus on the Cross. Oscar Romero had been asked to drink of the cup, just as Jesus had asked the sons of Zebedee, "Can you drink of the cup of which I am to drink?" (Mk 10:38). He had freely and knowingly chosen to do so. This is the true meaning of discipleship. Jesus asks the same question of each of his disciples. To answer in the affirmative is to be willing to suffer with him. If necessary, it means being ready to shed our own blood with him.

The ultimate sacrifice

Fr Andrew Bobola, a Polish Jesuit priest in 17th century, was called to share in the sacrifice of Jesus in a remarkable way.[49] In 1657 Pinsk was overrun by Cossacks, who were intent on cleansing the town of Catholics and forcing everyone to the Russian Orthodox faith. They arrested Fr Bobola and tried to persuade him to renounce his faith. He refused. In a mock passion they tied him to a hedge and began to whip him until blood flowed freely from his body. Already he was offering his blood in union with his Saviour. Then they placed a crown of thorns on his head and taunted him. Their savagery unsatisfied, they bound him behind two horses, and dragged him two miles to a neighbouring town. They took him to the butcher's shop, stretched him out on the butcher's table, and began their cruel torture. They tore his skin from his hands and head. Then in imitation of the chasuble the priest wears at Mass, they tore skin from his chest and back. Then in mock imitation of the wounds of Christ, they cut holes in the palms of his hands.

During the two hours of torture, Fr Bobola kept pleading aloud to the Lord for the souls of his captors. He also pleaded with his torturers to be concerned for their immortal souls. As with Jesus, he was not thinking of himself, even during such extreme agony. He was only thinking of the souls of his tormentors. They were so annoyed by this, they kept telling him to shut up. When he would not stop they eventually cut out his tongue. Like a piece of meat, they slammed an awl through his chest near the heart and strung him up by his feet. At last they gave him a final blow with a sabre that brought an end to his gruesome passion.

St Paul prayed that he be able "to share in the sufferings of Jesus by being able to imitate him in his death" (Phil 3:10). To follow Jesus means sharing in his passion. For Andrew Bobola it meant imitating the passion of Jesus literally. This was a wonderful sacrifice of love. During brutal torture he prayed for his enemies, with forgiveness in his heart. He shed his blood with Jesus for them. The sacrificial love of Jesus on Calvary was present on the butcher's table in the heart of the disciple. The ultimate test in life is not that we love those who we find pleasant and attractive, but that we love our enemies. Jesus said, "Love your enemies and pray for those who persecute you…" (Mt 5:43). This is what he came to show us by his sacrifice on the Cross; this is the love with which he empowers those who follow him.

8

Deliverance from Evil

He has rescued us from the power of darkness and transferred us into the kingdom of his beloved Son, in whom we have redemption, the forgiveness of sins. Col 1: 13-14

So far we have reflected on the tremendous love of the Savior pierced through on the Cross for our faults, and the reconciliation he has won by his blood cleansing us of sin. The focus has been on Good Friday. Yet we couldn't even have these liberating perspectives unless we had approached the Cross in the light of our faith in the Resurrection. As Paul says, "If Christ is not risen, our faith is in vain" (1Cor 15:14). The death and resurrection of Jesus are, as it were, two movements of the one symphony, or two acts of the one drama. They are two moments of the one decisive event that has brought our salvation. We proclaim, with Paul, that Christ "was put to death for our sins, and raised to life for our justification" (Rom 4:25). What would have been defeat and annihilation through Roman crucifixion, has now become victory and new life. The good news is that God the Father raised Jesus from the dead! This is what the apostles proclaimed so boldly and with utter conviction as they burst out of the upper room after the Holy Spirit had come upon them. Peter shouts aloud to the assembly, "You killed him, but God raised him to life, freeing him from Hades; for it was impossible for him to be held in its power" (Acts 2:23). Even in the Good Friday liturgy we recognize that the ultimate victory comes through the resurrection. A ninth-century antiphon for Good Friday says: "We adore your cross, Lord, and we praise your holy resurrection ... For behold on account of the wood of the cross joy has come into the whole world." Both the wood of the Cross and the wonder of the resurrection bring redemption to the world.

"Lifted up"

This unity of the cross and resurrection in the paschal mystery is illustrated powerfully in the liturgy for the feast of the Triumph of the Cross. The gospel of the day highlights Jesus being "lifted up" in the "hour" of his glorification: "Just as Moses lifted up the serpent in the desert in the wilderness, so must the Son of Man be lifted up, that whoever believes in him may have eternal life" (Jn 3:15). It refers to the time when the Israelites had been grumbling in the desert, and as a consequence were afflicted by fiery serpents bringing death to many. Moses cried out to God on behalf of the people. He was instructed by the Lord to make a bronzed serpent, fix it to a standard, and lift it up before the people. All who looked upon this image were delivered and healed.

Jesus looked forward to his being "lifted up" in the "hour" of his glorification. It is both a lifting up on the Cross of Calvary, and a lifting up by the Father into glory, through his resurrection and ascension. This is a powerful image, which holds together the two moments of the one paschal mystery. Later in the gospel, Jesus says to his opponents, who will be instrumental in his death, "When you have lifted up the Son of Man, then you will realize that I am He" (Jn 8:28). Here the emphasis is on our action of crucifying the Lord of glory. Jesus predicts that only after the crucifixion, when he is raised by the Father, will we be convinced of his true identity.

But the final usage of the phrase in John's gospel is the most revealing. Jesus was aware that his "hour" had come for "the Son of Man to be glorified" (Jn 12:23). He was not going to ask the Father to save him from this "hour" of his suffering and death, because the reason he had come to this "hour" was so that the Father would raise him from the dead. He says, "Now is judgment upon this world; now the ruler of this world will be driven out. And I, when I am lifted up from this earth, will draw all people to myself" (Jn 12:31-32). Jesus knew that the moment had come for the prince of darkness to be overthrown. When Jesus is "lifted up" on the Cross and by Resurrection, the rule of Satan will be decisively broken. This is the hour of his triumph over the power death and the Evil one.

Overcoming the kingdom of darkness

In the Synoptic gospels Jesus is presented in his public ministry as ushering in the Kingdom of God, and breaking the power of the evil one. In Mark's gospel he starts his ministry with a proclamation that sums up the whole of his mission, "The time has come, the Kingdom of God is upon you; repent and believe the good news" (Mk 1:14). In his person and actions Jesus is inaugurating the reign of God's power and love, the Kingdom of light, truth and mercy. Jesus was acutely aware that he was routing the kingdom of darkness, and breaking the stronghold of Satan and evil spirits. This is apparent in his preaching and healing ministry, and especially in his exorcisms. We only have to think of his dramatic deliverance of the Gerasene demoniac who had lived in tombs and had broken out of every chain or fetter that had been used to try to restrain him. The legions of evil spirits controlling him were cast out. Jesus taught his disciples to pray, "Deliver us from evil", and when the disciples returned from their first missionary journey they were full of joy, "Lord, in your name even the demons submit to us!" and Jesus replied, "See, I have given you authority to tread on snakes and scorpions, and over all the power of the enemy; and nothing will hurt you" (Lk 10:17-20).

Jesus explains the significance of his exorcisms, "If it is by the finger of God that I cast out demons, then the Kingdom of God is upon you" (Lk 11:20). Jesus had been confronted directly by Satan during his forty days in the desert. We are told he was tempted in every way that we are, but did not sin (Heb 2:18). His struggle in the desert was symbolic of his whole earthly journey. And his victory over Satan was definitive. Jesus has once and for all smashed Satan's power and delivered us from bondage to the enemy. "When a strong man fully armed guards his castle, his property is safe. But when one stronger than he attacks him and overpowers him, he takes away his armor in which he trusted and divides his plunder" (Lk 11:22).

Victory of the Cross

The climax of this battle with Satan occurred on the Cross. At the time of greatest tragedy, as the Son of God was nailed to the Cross, and left to die an ignominious death, it seemed the powers of darkness had won the victory. As Jesus had said to those who arrested him, "This is your hour; this is the reign of darkness" (Lk 22:53). It seemed that the evil powers had come out of their hiding place, and darkness reigned throughout the arrest, the trial, the condemnation and the crucifixion. But what appeared to be the case, was not the reality. What appeared to be the hour of victory for Satan, was the hour of his defeat. Love conquered hatred; goodness conquered evil. We saw in the previous chapter that God the Father suffered with Jesus during the passion; he willingly gave his Son over to death.

But Satan could not penetrate the plan of God, and was outwitted. From the outside it looked like a disaster. The apostles were in despairing grief, hiding in terror for fear of the people, lost and disorientated. What was left? A dead body in a tomb? Yes, but not for long. God, the Father raised him from the dead! This changed everything. Victory! As St Augustine said, "There is nothing special in believing that Jesus died: even pagans and the Jews and reprobates believe this; everyone believes it. The great thing is to believe that he rose from the dead. The faith of Christians is the resurrection of Christ."[50] Without the resurrection how would we have known the true meaning of Christ's death? The resurrection is God the Father's "yes" to the offering of Jesus in sacrifice; it is the assurance that the life and death of Jesus truly brings salvation. By dying, Jesus said "yes" to the Father, being obedient unto death; by raising Jesus from the dead, the Father said "yes" to the Son, making him Lord.

The theme of Jesus as the Victor King over the powers of sin, death and Satan was a favourite with the early Fathers of the Church. They drew upon the rich New Testament revelation that the risen Christ reigns forever. Death could not hold him down. Previously physical death was a tragedy without hope, and spiritual death due to sin was a helpless pit. Now Paul can sing: "Death has been swallowed up in victory. Where, O death, is your victory? Where, O death, is your sting? The sting of death is sin… But thanks be to God, who gives us the victory through our Lord Jesus Christ" (1Cor 15:54-57). Jesus had come as the humble Lamb taken to the slaughter, but now "the Lamb who was slain has victory gained." In Revelations the Lamb, still carrying the wounds of his sacrifice, is the Victory over all evil: "Worthy is the Lamb that was slain to receive power and wealth and wisdom and might and honour and glory and blessing … to the one seated on the throne and to the Lamb be blessing and honour and glory and might forever and ever!" (Rev 5:12-14).

The Passover mystery

At the Easter Vigil celebration it is mandatory to include the epic story of the crossing of the Red Sea which evokes the imagery of the Passover. All the symbolism is of the victorious God of Israel who rescued his people from the evil of Pharoah's enslavement, and brought them miraculously through the waters of the Red Sea to deliverance. The "Passover" was not only the prefiguration of the passion of Jesus, symbolized by the paschal Lamb eaten in haste before the Israelites set out on their journey. It was also interpreted by St Augustine as the "passing over" of Jesus to the Father, which speaks of both his death and his resurrection. "For by his passion the

Lord passed from death to life and made a way for us who believe in his resurrection, so that we too may pass from death to life."[51]

This passage through the Red Sea had become, even before Augustine, a symbol for Christian baptism. The baptized are immersed into the death and resurrection of Jesus, which brings victory over sin and freedom from enslavement to Satan. Just as Jesus has "passed over" to the Father, so we who are immersed into his death and resurrection in Baptism "pass over" from death to life in Him. The Vigil celebration always includes the classic hymn by which Moses and the people praised God for their deliverance from Egypt:

> I will sing to the Lord, for he has triumphed gloriously; horse and rider he has thrown into the sea. The Lord is my strength and my might, and he has become my salvation…The Lord is a warrior; the Lord is his name. Pharoah's chariots and his army he cast into the sea … Your right hand, O lord, glorious in power – your right hand, O Lord, shattered the enemy. (Ex.15: 1-2, 3-4.6)

We sing this song of victory at Easter not only because we remember what God has done for his people of old; but also because we celebrate what he has done for us in the new Passover, giving us victory over the power of sin, death and Satan, and lifting us with him into fullness of light and life.

Ransom for the many

Another strong biblical image of redemptive deliverance is that Christ paid the ransom owing to our sins. Jesus told us he came "to give his life as a ransom for the many" (Mk 10:45). Paul says "There is one God and there is one mediator between God and man, the man Christ Jesus, who gave himself as a ransom for all" (1Tim 2:5-6). And First Peter reminds us, "Remember the ransom that was paid to free you from the useless way of life your ancestors handed down was not paid in anything corruptible, neither in silver nor in gold, but in the precious blood of the lamb without spot and stain, namely Christ" (1 Pet 1:18-19).

Some of the early Fathers took this analogy to the extreme and depicted our enslavement to evil as being in bondage to the devil, who had rights of ownership over us. Thus, Jesus had to pay a high price by the shedding of his blood to purchase us back from Satan. This was an unfortunately literal way of dealing with the metaphor. The idea of a transaction with the devil was vigorously resisted by some, but it held widespread popularity. However, this was not Paul's point at all. He was accustomed to the ancient practice that slaves could be "redeemed"; they could theoretically win their freedom, by obtaining enough money equivalent to their purchase price. But this was practically impossible for them. They were helpless to do anything for themselves. Their only chance for freedom would be if some wealthy person gratuitously took mercy on them and paid the purchase price. This would be an extravagantly lavish act of kindness and goodness, which would leave the former slave forever grateful.

In using this image Paul was focusing on who paid the price, and how costly it really was. We had been enslaved to sin and under the power of Satan. When we were helpless to do anything about it, God acted through the passion, death and resurrection of Jesus, to win our freedom. It was very costly, since it meant the Son of God suffering, and dying for us in order to win our redemption. There was no "deal" with Satan. Rather by the power of the blood that was shed, and by the mighty hand of the Father raising Jesus from the dead, Satan's dominion was shattered. We have been rescued from Satan's grip and are now God's possession. Paul reminds the Corinthians, "You were bought with a price; therefore glorify God in your body" (1 Cor 6:20). In other words, God went to enormous lengths, out of love, to gain possession of us. This should make us realize how uniquely prized we are in his eyes, and what dignity he has given us since we belong to him. This image has its origins in the Old Testament where the redeeming action of God freed the people from slavery to their enemies, but also made them his very own, consecrated people. The

Lord says, "Do not be afraid, for I have redeemed you; I have called you by name, you are mine" (Is 43:1).

A parable of deliverance

In the days of slave-trading a young woman had been captured in Africa and forced onto a slave ship bound for a South American port. On arrival at the port, shackled with heavy chains, she stood trembling in the public auction. She was the next slave to be purchased by the highest bidder. The bidding began; a hundred dollars ... three hundred ... five hundred ... Then a bid from an unknown figure down the back ... one million dollars! No one had ever bid so much for a common slave. The gavel fell. The mysterious new owner claimed his purchase, and led her outside, where they were alone. She was terrified. Then she saw the look in his eyes – such goodness and kindness she had never experienced before. To her astonishment, this gracious man took out a key from his pocket and unlocked her chains. They fell to the ground. He said, "You are free now. You may go if you wish." For a moment she stood in stunned silence. Then she ran, and ran, until she was too tired to run any more. Exhausted, she slumped on the grass in a field. Then she began to think of the goodness and kindness of her liberator. With new energy she rose and slowly made her way back. He was waiting for her, and greeted her with a welcoming smile. She said, "I would love to work in your household. You have been so good to me. In gratitude I will happily place myself in your service". He accepted.

Jesus, our Saviour, because of his love, has purchased us from slavery to Satan by the shedding of his blood, and has freed us from the chains that had kept us in bondage. In gratitude, we offer our service to him as Lord and Master of our lives.

Reality of evil

Some theologians dismiss this concept of deliverance from the forces of darkness as far-fetched. They dismiss the New Testament description of demons as ancient mythology; medieval in outlook and irrelevant today. There are two dangers of talking in extremes about the spiritual powers of darkness. The first is to overstate the activity of evil spirits, as if there was "an evil spirit under every bush". Too much attention to Satan can prove fatal, and is never a healthy perspective. The second danger is more today's problem – the tendency to deny the existence of evil spirits, or at least to downplay their activity as a bit of spooky fun. People who espouse this notion, seem to be blind to the consummate evil evidenced in human atrocities such as the Pol Pot regime in Thailand, the ethnic massacre in Rwanda, the thousands eliminated during the Bosnian war; and we could go on forever reporting hatred, torture, rape, serial murder, and the countless massacres of innocent people. The blatant insanity and destructiveness of so much that is truly good points towards a personal power of evil behind it all.

The teaching of the Church is that Satan and evil spirits were created by God as angels. At some point these pure spirits rebelled against God and fell. They now hate God and are totally dedicated to the destruction of the work of God (CC 391-393). Pope Paul VI once asked the question: "What are the greatest needs of the Church today?" He gave a somewhat sobering answer:

> Do not let our answer surprise you as being over simple or even superstitious and unreal: one of the greatest needs is defence from that evil which is called the Devil. Evil is not merely a lack of something, but an effective agent, a living spiritual being, perverted and perverting. A terrible reality. It is contrary to the teaching of the Church to refuse to recognize the existence of such a reality... or to explain it as a pseudo reality, a conceptual and fanciful personification of the unknown causes of our misfortunes.[52]

Until the death and resurrection of Jesus mankind was helplessly in the grip of Satan. Now through the death and resurrection of Jesus, Satan has been dealt a decisive blow. He has lost the battle. Christ has won the victory. Through our baptism the redemptive work of Jesus' death and resurrection has been applied to our lives, and we celebrate it in each Eucharist. Blessed John Paul II put it so splendidly:

> When we are shaken by the sight of evil spreading in the universe, with all the devastation which it produces, we should not forget that such unleashing of the forces of sin is overcome by the saving power of Christ. Whenever the words of consecration are uttered in the Mass and the body and blood of Christ become present in the act of sacrifice, the triumph of love over hatred, of holiness over sin is also present. Every Eucharistic celebration is stronger than all the evil in the universe; it means real, concrete accomplishment of the Redemption, an ever deeper reconciliation of sinful man with God, in prospect of a better world.[53]

There is more power available to us for good in every Eucharist celebrated devoutly than in all the evil in the universe. The victory has been won, and can never be reversed. But in the mystery of God's ways the redemption is not yet complete.

The spiritual battle

The spiritual battle still rages. Evil spirits are still operative. Probably their most devastating work is not in the more overt manifestations of evil mentioned above, but rather in the deceptive, seductive work of tempting good people to do wrong things. The Enemy wants to keep this hidden work under wraps. Satan's vehemence against God makes him the enemy of our human nature, and we would be foolish to underestimate what a formidable foe he is. On the other hand we have no reason to fear. The victory has been won. The Risen Christ reigns now and he has put all of his enemies under his feet. In Ephesians Paul prays that we would come to know the "immeasurable greatness" of God's power in us who believe. He says, "God put this power to work in Christ when he raised him from the dead and seated him at his right hand in the heavenly places, far above all rule and authority and power and dominion, and above every name that is named... And he has put all things under his feet and has made him the head over all things ..." (Eph 1: 20-22).

In proclaiming the victory we need to be realists, but *optimistic* realists. Some may think that it is too facile and superficial to proclaim the victory over evil in the world when hatred, ethnic cleansing, widespread abortion, war, greed and enforced poverty exist. The answer to this is that we live in a state of *already* being redeemed, but we have *not yet* reached its consummation. We live in between the first coming of Christ, who has redeemed us from sin and Satan, and the second coming of the Lord when he will bring his work to completion. Jesus has definitively won the conclusive victory over evil: "It was to undo all that the devil has done that the Son of God appeared" (Jn 3:8). Paul says, "He disarmed the rulers and authorities and made a public example of them, triumphing over them in it" (Col 2:15). Paul is using an image of the way captive soldiers were stripped of their arms and paraded in public as they were brought back to Rome in procession behind the triumphant General. That is how Christ the Victor has dealt with his enemies. The First Letter of Peter concurs: through his resurrection "Jesus Christ has gone into heaven and is at the right hand of God, with angels, authorities and powers made subject to him" (1 Pet 3:22).

But the full out-working of Christ's redemption is yet to come. Paul says, "For Christ must reign until he has put all his enemies under his feet. The last enemy to be destroyed is death" (1 Cor 15:25-26). Paul is acknowledging that while death does not have to destroy us any more, it still must be undergone until the final resurrection from the dead. When Christ cried out on the Cross just before he died, "It is accomplished!" (Jn 19:30), this was the truth. All that needed to be done for our salvation has been done through his death and resurrection. Nothing more has to be accomplished. However, it has to be worked through in human history, and will only be brought to completion at the end of time. We have all been baptized in Christ, immersed into the power of his death and resurrection. We have all received the Spirit of adoption making us sons and daughters of God and a new creation in Christ. Yet we still groan within us, together with the whole of creation, for the full redemption yet to come (Rom 8:19-25).

For now Satan still remains a formidable opponent. We are warned, "Like a roaring lion your adversary the devil prowls around looking for someone to devour. Resist him, steadfast in your faith" (1 Pet 5:8-9). We are not mere spectators to the cosmic victory of Christ over the powers of evil. We are meant to be active participants. We must say "yes" to what has been accomplished for us. We do this by repentance, faith and baptism. And we must engage in the on-going spiritual battle. Paul says, "You know what time it is, how it is now the moment to wake from sleep. For salvation is nearer to us now than when we became believers; the night is far gone, the day is near. Let us then lay aside the works of darkness and put on the armour of light.." He urges to get rid of all sinful ways and complicity with the powers of darkness, and "put on the Lord Jesus Christ, making no provision for the flesh, to gratify your desires" (Rom 13:11-14).

Paul assures us that the Lord himself will supply the armour we need for the spiritual battle. "Put on the whole armour of God, so that you may be able to stand against the wiles of the devil" (Eph 6:11-17). Our struggle he warns is not against "flesh and blood"; that is, not against other human beings. Rather it is against "the cosmic powers of the present darkness, against the spiritual forces of evil in the heavenly places." Using imagery from the armour of Roman soldiers, Paul tells us what we need for the battle. Firstly, the "belt of truth around your waist". Humility is truth, and this is what holds everything together. Next is the "breastplate of righteousness"; being right with God, but also being right with others. The pursuit of holiness in love and justice is a good protection of the heart. Next is having the shoes of "readiness to proclaim the gospel of peace". Eagerness to proclaim the Good News is the best protection from the evil one. That is why Jesus promised the Church that in proclamation of the Good News, which is the essence of the Church's mission, "the gates of hell will not prevail against it" (Mt 16:18).

Then there is the "shield of faith" to stop the flaming arrows of the evil one. We remember that the Roman army advanced with shields the height of a soldier locked together, and sometimes raised high together to deflect the fiery darts of the enemy. The faith we share in the Church is our protection; being one with the faith of the Church expressed especially in its teaching authority. Then there is the "helmet of salvation". This is a call to guard the mind against the incursions of the enemy. The mind should be rooted in the truth of our redemption won by the crucified Lord. We know that the victory has been won by the Cross of Jesus. It has been applied to our lives by Baptism, and renewed often in Eucharist. We need to have an active mind, filling it with everything that is good, true, beautiful and holy (Phil 4:8). We are also to have ready the "sword of the Spirit", which is the word of God. This is primarily a reference to the Scriptural word, that we should memorize, and have ready to use against any attack from the evil one. Finally Paul exhorts us to pray in the Spirit on every possible occasion, praying not only for ourselves but for others. Without perseverance in prayer we are an open target for the designs of the evil one.

9
Resurrection: Our Hope

Filled with awe and great joy the women came quickly away from the tomb and ran to tell the disciples. And there, coming to meet them, was Jesus Mt 28:8.

One could easily get the impression that for Catholics in the Western tradition Good Friday is where all the action is. Easter Sunday is just a happy sequel to the main event, and almost an afterthought in the mind of preachers and theologians. Nothing could be further from the truth. To correct any imbalance in our thinking I want to dedicate one chapter simply to the significance of the Resurrection in our lives. Seraphim Sarov, one of the Russian saints, after being for ten years in solitude in a forest, simply soaking himself in Christ, emerged from his experience transformed. People would flock to his monastery, and he would greet them with the words, "My joy, Christ is risen!" That was enough to convert their hardened hearts.

The object of our resurrection faith is not the empty tomb, even though this is a crucial fact that we know to be true. Rather, our faith is in the risen Christ himself. What changed the apostles was when they met the Lord still carrying his wounds. He had been raised into glory, shot through with the Spirit. Not a resuscitated corpse like Lazarus had been. Lazarus died again. But for Jesus death has no power over him anymore. He is alive! He is Lord! The apostles had trouble recognizing him at first, because while he was definitely the same Jesus of Nazareth, now he walked through walls. He was changed into glory. Yet the gospel writers were keen to testify it was the same Jesus – they touched him, they saw his wounds, he ate with them. But now, things were different. They were to return to Galilee, but not back to the old routine of discipleship. They were to go to meet him there as the risen Lord. To become a disciple now was *to first encounter the Risen Christ*, to know him by faith.

Thomas, who had doubted, was given a special appearance, and an opportunity to touch the wounds of Jesus. That touch must have electrified Thomas. He was on his knees, "My Lord and my God!" (Jn 20:28). Adoration was the only appropriate response. Jesus said to Thomas, "You believe because you have seen, blessed are those who have not seen and yet believe!" (Jn 20:29). That means us. Our encounter with the risen Christ is no less real than that of Thomas. It is as if the lights go on inside us for the first time. Paul described the experience. He said it is like when God said at the beginning of time, "Let there be light!" In a similar way he has turned on the light of faith in our hearts. "He has shone in our hearts to give the light of the knowledge of the glory of God in the face of Jesus Christ" (2 Cor 4:6).

Power to change

When you think of the incredible energy and power in the universe it boggles the mind. Scientists tell us that in the Sun, which is a relatively small body in the whole universe, the equivalent of hundreds of hydrogen bombs explode every second. That's hard to get our minds around. But we Christians proclaim that there is a new explosive power in the universe much greater than anything that can be investigated by science. Paul uses this word "power" often. The Greek word is *dunamis*, from which we get the words "dynamic", and "dynamite". It is the dynamic, explosive, power manifest in the resurrection of Christ. Paul prays, "that the God of our Lord Jesus Christ, the Father of glory, may give you a spirit of wisdom and revelation as you come to know him, so that, with the eyes of your heart enlightened, you may come to know … what is the immeasurable greatness of his *power* for us who believe … God put his *power* to work in Christ when he raised him from the dead and seated him at his right hand ..." (Eph 1:17-20). What is this power? It is the power to change, the power to become a whole new creation in Christ. Elsewhere Paul exclaimed, "all I want is to know Jesus Christ and the power of his resurrection ..." (Phil 3:10).

No longer do we have to walk through life feeling defeated by patterns of sin, and threatened by forces within us and outside of us that seem to hold us back. The Good News of the resurrection gives us new hope. When the Father raised Jesus from the dead he fulfilled his promise. The Father together with Jesus at his right hand, sent the Holy Spirit to make of us a new creation. Later in Ephesians Paul prays that "you may be strengthened in your inner being by the power of his Holy Spirit" and then at the end of the prayer cries, "Glory be to him whose power within us can do infinitely more than we can ask or imagine" (Eph 3:20).

This should give us enormous confidence in the fight against sin. We have the victory of Jesus already applied to our lives in baptism. Paul tells us that when we were baptized we were joined with Jesus in his death. It is as if we went into the tomb with him. But Jesus was raised from the tomb by the Father in the power of the Holy Spirit. So in baptism we too were joined with Jesus in his resurrection. Paul says, "When Christ died, he died once for all, to sin, so his life now is life with God; and in that way, you too must consider yourselves to be dead to sin but alive for God in Christ Jesus" (Rom 6:11). This is the Good News! Sin does not have to dominate our lives anymore. Such is the mercy of our God!

Paul was no doubt familiar with the Genesis account of the first creation. The breath of God, the "Ruah", or Spirit, hovered over the chaos, bringing order and new life. The same Spirit hovered over the dead body of Jesus, and the Father raised him from the dead to be the "first fruits" of the new creation. This Holy Spirit now lives in us. We have unlimited power to be able to change. Paul says, "If the

Spirit of him who raised Jesus from the dead dwells in you, he who raised Christ from the dead will give life to your mortal bodies also through his Spirit that dwells in you" (Rom 8:11). When Paul speaks of giving "life to your mortal bodies" he is not only referring to the resurrection of the body on the last day. He means our historical existence right now. Christ is risen in our hearts by the Spirit given to us, and this is our hope. This resurrection power gives us the energy to live as a new creation. As he says elsewhere, "So if anyone is in Christ, there is a new creation: everything old has passed away; see, everything has become new!" (2 Cor 5:17).

There is now a new power and a new energy in the universe that scientists, New-Agers, and philosophers of this age know nothing about. It has come through the resurrection of Jesus Christ. If the first creation began with a Big Bang, as some scientists would have us believe, the new creation began with an even greater explosion of power, when Jesus rose into glory. Because he is risen, we no longer have to be enslaved to our bodily passions, or to our disordered emotions and thoughts. We have been given new life through the waters of baptism. Paul says, "You have been buried with him when you were baptized; and by baptism, too, you have been raised with him through your belief in the power of God who raised him from the dead. You were dead because you were sinners…he has brought you to life with him" (Col 2:12-13).

How can this resurrection power, given to us in the Spirit, take effect in our lives? In faith we must appropriate the grace of our baptism. We must give our personal "yes" to what has been done by Christ. We must repent of our sin, acknowledge Jesus as the Saviour and Lord of our lives. We must surrender to the power of the Holy Spirit. We must consciously take hold of the grace of our baptism. Paul is constantly reminding his communities that they have been already given everything they need for their salvation and their sanctification. He reminds them, "When the goodness and loving kindness of our Saviour appeared, he saved us, not because of any works of righteousness we had done, but according to his mercy, through the water of rebirth and the renewal by the Holy Spirit" (Titus 3:5). Because this grace has already been given us, which we have not deserved, we must no longer cling to our old ways of thinking and acting. We must change our lives, drawing upon the power given to us in Christ: "You must give up your old way of life; you must put aside your old self, which gets corrupted by following illusory desires. Your mind must be renewed by a spiritual revolution, so that you can put on the new self that has been created in God's way, in the goodness and holiness of the truth" (Eph 4:22-24).

Children of the Father

When the early Christians began to proclaim Jesus is risen they did not first speak about the resurrection as something that Christ had done. Rather, they first proclaimed that it was the work of the Almighty Father. They declared, "God raised him from the dead" and to describe the Father's joy, they used the text, "You are my Son, today I have begotten you" (Acts 13:33). It was a celebration of the begetting of the Son by the Father from all eternity. The resurrection is a gift of the Father to his Beloved Son in whom he is well pleased. After all the excruciating agony of the passion and death, now the Father breaks his "silence" and raises Christ to be seated at his right hand in glory. This is the pinnacle of all of God's saving action in history. Now the God of Abraham, Isaac and Jacob has revealed himself to be much more. From now on he is to be acclaimed as "He who raised Jesus Christ from the dead" (cf. 2 Cor 4:14; Gal 1:1; Col 2:12). In resurrection Jesus rejoined his Father who is love. He "was proclaimed Son of God in all his power through his resurrection from the dead" (Rom 1:4).

Understanding the resurrection as the Father's gift to the Son has enormous consequences for us. With the fulfillment of the promise of the outpouring of the Holy Spirit we have become sons and daughters of God "in the Son". Paul says, "Blessed be God the Father of our Lord Jesus Christ who has blessed us with all the spiritual blessings from heaven in Christ … determining that we should become his adopted sons (daughters) …" (Eph 1:3). All the resurrection power bestowed on Christ has been bestowed on us as well. Through baptism the Holy Spirit has made us sons and daughters, able to call God, "Abba", Father. The very way of intimately addressing the Father which was used exclusively by Jesus, the Beloved Son, is now for us to use as well. "The proof that you are sons (daughters) is that God has sent the Spirit of his Son into our hearts: the Spirit that cries, "Abba, Father", and it is this that makes you a son (daughter), you are not a slave anymore; and if God has made you son (daughter), then he has made you heir" (Gal 4:6-7; cf. Rom 8:14-17). We have been drawn into the relationship between the Father and the Son by the indwelling of the Holy Spirit. This establishes our identity in God. Fear cannot dominate us anymore. We know the freedom of the sons and daughters of God. Knowing oneself to be the "beloved son" or the "beloved daughter" of the Father anchors us in our true worth and dignity. It brings meaning to our lives, and confidence that no matter how chaotic life may become, we are held in his unconditional love and protected by the infinite power of the Father.

Resurrection hope

Through the resurrection of Jesus we have a "sure hope" that will never fail us. Resurrection speaks of the faithfulness of God the Father, who raised Jesus from the dead. In raising Jesus from the dead the Father gave the ultimate proof that Jesus is the Son of God, as he had claimed to be. But while that in itself was marvellous, the Father gave us much more. He gave us a "living hope"; the resurrection is not just a demonstration of the truth of Christianity, it is also a power that nourishes hope in the heart.

"Blessed be the God and Father of our Lord Jesus Christ! By his great mercy he has given us a new birth into *a living hope* through the resurrection of Jesus Christ from the dead" (1 Pet 1:3). This hope is not simply "wishful thinking." In common parlance we might say "I hope it doesn't rain tomorrow". But we have no guarantee that it won't rain. It is conjectural thinking. "Maybe it will happen". This is not how it is with Christian hope. Our hope is rooted in Christ. It is founded on the sure knowledge of the reality and majesty of the Risen Christ. We are sure that the resurrection of the body will take place on the last day. And we are sure that through faith we can experience his resurrection in our hearts now.

Our hope is based on an historical event; something that actually happened in history. There were no earthly creatures present to witness the event. But the witness of the apostles of their encounters with the Risen Christ before his ascension leaves no doubt of its historicity. Add to that the reality of the empty tomb; "the stone was rolled away". And then there was the extraordinary explosion of fearless preaching leading to the miraculous expansion of the Church. All of this evidence leaves little doubt that it actually happened. Yet it was an event that also transcended history. God the Father gave his answer of love to the Son's sacrifice of love, by raising him from the dead in the power of the Spirit. It was a Trinitarian event.

But our living hope is not only founded on the apostolic witness. It is based in our own real, personal encounter with the reality and majesty of the Risen Christ. The object of our faith is not primarily in the empty tomb, but in the Risen Lord himself. Faith, by its nature, is a divine gift which brings certitude. Paul reminds the Ephesians how, before coming to know Christ, they "were immersed in the world without hope and without God" (Eph 2:12). Unfortunately that is the situation of many in the world today. Without God there is no genuine hope for any human being. When we actually know the love of God revealed in Jesus Christ we have a guarantee that he will never abandon us. Paul says, "Hope does not disappoint us, because God's love has been poured into our hearts through the Holy Spirit who has been given to us" (Rom 5:5).

Our hope is not only for future glory, but is the foundation of our life now. It is the gift of "eternal life" which we experience now, and will be brought to fullness when we die. Jesus promised: "I came that they may have life, and have it abundantly" (Jn 10:10). It is not just for heaven, and not only for the resurrection on the last day, but *for now*. Our great hope that stands firm, despite whatever disappointments we face, is the sure knowledge that God the Father is faithful. He raised Jesus Christ from the dead. And we now live in Christ by the power of the Spirit who is the pledge and guarantee of a "future full of hope" (Jer 29:11). Paul encourages us to take hold of the truth that we are "in Christ" through the power of the Spirit. We have a new hope that will never let us down. He prays that we may come to full knowledge of God the Father, who raised Jesus from the dead: "May he enlighten the eyes of your mind so that you can see what hope his call holds for you, what rich glories he has promised the saints will inherit…" (Eph 1:18).

No matter what dark tomb we have in our lives – loneliness, addiction, rejection, a shattered sense of self-worth – whatever it is – Jesus wants to be with us in that pain, and burst us out of that tomb. He will bring his Risen light into the darkest place in the heart, and fill it. He will break us out of any interior prison. He will burst us out of any self-made tomb, or a tomb that seems to have been forced on us by others. He has come to save us. We too can sing with joy, "I know that my Redeemer lives!" And, because of this we can also sing, "I know that I have come to life in Him!" All we need to do is welcome him fully into our hearts. Let him be Lord!

Christ breaks the chains

In the small village of Medjugorje in Bosnia-Hercegovina the Virgin Mary is believed to have been appearing to young people since

1981. The village has become a centre of pilgrimage and a place of many conversions. At the foot of the Hill of Apparitions there is a community of young men called *Cenacolo*. The members of the community are young men who are undergoing a unique recovery program from drug addiction. Prayer before the Blessed Sacrament, and work on a stone quarry make up the day. They are called to repent and believe the Good News. The testimonies of those delivered from bondage to drugs are profoundly moving. They witness to the liberating power of the Risen Christ, who in the Spirit went to visit those in darkness and who "shattered the doors of bronze and cut in two the bars of iron" (Ps 107:16).

To celebrate their deliverance the brothers of *Cenacolo* prayed and fasted for weeks before some of the more talented ones painted a giant icon on the wall of their chapel behind the altar. The icon depicts a classic scene from the Eastern tradition. The Risen Christ is the centre piece. He is rising out of the tomb triumphantly. But he is not by himself. He is drawing behind him Adam and Eve, and all the patriarchs and prophets of the Old Testament, and then presumably all of us who have been saved. In the picture Christ has just obviously come from the descent into hell, because the chains of darkness are clearly broken. The whole scene depicts the victory of the Risen Christ over sin, death, and the powers of darkness. It proclaims the hope that Christ brings to all who turn to him. The young men of *Cenacolo* testify to experiencing this victory. They say, "Those chains you see broken are what has happened to us". Their lives and their radiant faces are a sign of the radiant hope that Christ brings to all who turn to him, and repent, and believe in his saving power.

10

Jesus is Lord

Do not be afraid; it is I, the First and the Last; I am the Living One. I was dead and now I am to live for ever and ever, and I hold the keys of death and of the underworld. Rev 1:17

All the preaching and teaching of Jesus of Nazareth, and all his healings and exorcisms, proclaimed a single message, "The time has come, the kingdom of God is upon you!" In his person and his ministry Jesus announced the rule of God's love breaking into history; and he called all to respond, "Repent and believe the Good News" (Mk 1:15).

In the preaching of the early Church, the language of "the kingdom" was not so prominent. Yet, the apostles preached what God had done in Jesus of Nazareth. They shouted from the rooftops, "Jesus is Lord!" By this they meant that in Jesus, now crucified and risen, the kingdom and sovereignty of God has been established. They were affirming that "the power, honor and glory due to God the Father are due also to Jesus" (CC 449).

In the Greek translation of the Old Testament, which was used in the early Church, the title of "YHWH", which God revealed to Moses at the burning bush, was rendered as "Kurios", "Lord". So when the early Christians proclaimed "Jesus is Lord!" they were recognizing him as God. When Thomas finally encounters the Risen Jesus, he falls in adoration, "My Lord and my God!" In Philippians Paul gives us an ancient hymn, which declares, "God highly exalted him and gave him the name that is above every other name, so that at the name of Jesus, every knee should bow, in heaven and on earth, and every tongue confess that *Jesus Christ is Lord* to the glory of God the Father" (Phil 2:9-11).

Jesus, who is Lord and Master, is "the key, the centre, and the purpose of the whole of man's history" (GS 10, 3). He is the Alpha and the Omega, the beginning and end of everything. All powers are subject to him. In the Roman Empire it was customary to call Caesar "kurios", or "lord", and it was incumbent upon all subjects to worship the Emperor. The early Christians were adamant that they would not submit their freedom in an absolute manner to any earthly power. They would only bow in worship of God the Father and the Lord Jesus Christ. The Book of Revelations is forthright in its proclamation: "The kingdom of the world has become the Kingdom of our Lord, and of his Christ, and he will reign forever and ever" (Rev 11:15).

Faith in the Risen Lord

It is not enough to know about what God has accomplished for us in Jesus Christ. We may have learnt about it all in the catechism, but not have truly appropriated it in our lives. Faith is the door into the kingdom. We don't enter the kingdom through doing good works, nor do we enter the kingdom by keeping the commandments, nor do we enter the kingdom by having virtue. We enter by faith in Christ, by accepting him as my Saviour and Lord. Paul says: "If you confess with your lips that Jesus is Lord, and believe in your heart that God raised him from the dead you shall be saved" (Rom 10:9). Do we "believe in the heart"?

Many people in the Church are like the two men on the road to Emmaus. They were walking away from Jerusalem, detaching themselves from the saving event of Christ's death and resurrection. For them it had not brought hope, but despair. Their faces were downcast. All was doom and gloom as they commiserated with one another. The Risen Jesus was with them but they did not recognize him. When he probed them about their misery, they tell a story which for them offered no hope. Yet the story contained all the facts of the kerygma. They had seen the miracles of Jesus, they had witnessed his passion and death, and they had heard reports that he had risen. Yet the Good News had not connected with them personally. They needed revelation from on high, the gift of supernatural faith. Their hearts began to burn within them as Jesus spoke the word to them. Finally their "eyes were opened" in "the breaking of the bread". The eyes of faith need to be opened for many today so they too can know personally the Risen Christ and realize what he has done for us.

Justified by faith

Paul writes to the Romans, "Now the righteousness of God has been revealed" (Rom 3:21). By 'righteousness' he means the goodness and mercy of God who has come to save us in Christ. Paul tells us that God the Father put Jesus forward as a sacrifice on the Cross in order "to prove at the present time that he himself is righteous and that he justifies the one who has faith in Jesus" (Rom 3:26). We are personally made right with God by faith in Jesus. Both Jesus' preaching of the kingdom, and Paul's preaching that Jesus is Lord, call for a response of conversion and faith. The only appropriate response to what Jesus has accomplished for us through his Cross and resurrection is to turn from sinful ways and to turn our lives over fully to God (1 Thess 1:9).

Some people in the Church may still be laboring under the burden of the law. Possibly they still feel that they have to make their own way to God. Only if they can change their lives, and live by the commandments, then they will be found pleasing to God. If they clean up their act by their own efforts, then God will come to save them. They are trying to climb up the ladder of perfection, seeking to perform well before a demanding God. Often they experience dismal failure to achieve their goals, and are weighed down by shame and guilt. They spend their energy on a religious tread-mill of their own making, or maybe they just give up in quiet despair.

This religious syndrome is bondage, because it is an attempt to attain righteousness by our own efforts. It was the problem of the Pharisees in the Gospels. They could not appreciate that the Kingdom of God preached by Jesus was a gift of God's saving love. We cannot earn it. Any merit we happen to gain in life is only an expression of what has already been given to us. Rather than trying to prove ourselves before God, we need to realize that God has proved his love to us. He has done this in sending his only Son, who died to pay the debt owing to our sin, and is now risen and glorified. As John says, "This is the love I mean: not our love for God, but God's love for us, when he sent his Son to be the sacrifice which takes our sins away" (1 Jn 4:10).

Paul knew the Pharisaical enslavement to the law more than anyone. He had been an exemplary Pharisee. But after encountering the Risen Christ on the road to Damascus he no longer wanted "a righteousness of my own coming from the law, but that which comes through faith in Christ." He says, "I want only to know Christ and the power of his resurrection ..." (Phil 3:9). Paul no longer felt compelled to strive for perfection by his own efforts. Through faith he had received, as sheer gift, the righteousness that comes from Christ.

Open the door to Christ

The call to "repent" and to "believe" are two moments of the one response to the Good News of Jesus Christ. We must turn from sin, and turn to Jesus as our Saviour and Lord. We are invited to open wide the door of the heart to Jesus Christ.

> Be earnest, therefore, and repent. Listen, I am standing at the door, knocking; if you hear my voice and open the door, I will come in to you and eat with you, and you with me". (Rev 3:19-20)

There is a famous Hans Holbein painting of Christ standing before a door, which is overgrown with vegetation. The door has obviously not been opened for some time. Christ holds a lantern, representing the light he wants to bring into the darkness within. Admirers of the painting often remark that the artist forgot to paint a handle on the door. How else can Christ open it? But this omission by the artist was deliberate. The point is simple. The door of the heart has no outside handle. There is only an *inside* handle, by which only we can open the door. Christ continues to knock, but he leaves us free to open or not. He does not force his way into our lives. We must make a "yes" to what he has accomplished for us through his saving love. Only we can open the door and let him enter, and accept his gift of love and friendship.

God created us to be in obedience to him. He made us free to accept the gracious gift of life and love. He was waiting for our "yes". Instead he received a "no". Now God has offered us a second chance, which will bring us a new creation. He has given us Christ, our Redeemer. He asks us, "Will you allow Christ to live in you as your Saviour and Lord?"; "Will you choose to ratify the truth of your baptism and live in Christ, and submit to him as your Lord?" When we say "yes" we become a new creation, which far surpasses the first creation (2 Cor 5:17).

We don't have to worry about making ourselves right with God. Deep in the heart of all of us there is an innate feeling that we have to "pay God his price", that we have to first make satisfaction for our sins before he will forgive[54], that we have to win our salvation, that we have to merit our entry into eternal life.[55] Hidden under this attitude is a pridefulness, a penchant for autonomy, a desire to do it myself – nothing less than the perennial sin of disobedience which messed up the human race in the first place. The gift of salvation in Christ is totally gratuitous. Our response is to bow before him and humbly accept this precious gift of the Kingdom. It is a response of deep gratitude for a gift we did not deserve, and could not have attained. Paul says, "For by grace you have been saved through faith, and this is not your own doing; it is the gift of God – not the result of works, so that no one may boast" (Eph 2:8).

Why does the Lord keep hammering away in Scripture that it is all God's gift? Because he does not want us boasting about anything. That was where things went wrong in the first creation. Now in the new creation we need to be aware that all we have received is by grace in Jesus Christ. Paul says, "God is the source of your life in Christ Jesus, who became for us wisdom from God, and righteousness, and sanctification and redemption" (1 Cor 1:30). Christ is our righteousness. His power within us makes us right with God, and brings us fullness of life. I don't have to try to make myself virtuous by straining under the pressure of the law, or my pushing myself stoically towards an ideal of perfection through exerting my own will power. I simply have to yield my whole self, give my mind and my will, and all that I am to Christ Jesus, my Lord.

Let Christ be Lord

Jesus wants to be Lord of our whole life, not just part of it. This is the only way he can truly be our friend. He says, "You are my friends if you do what I command you" (Jn 15:14). Many want to be friends with Jesus on their own terms. But this would be to try to reverse the right order of things. Intimacy with Jesus is the greatest treasure of all, but it can only be had through a genuine submission of one's life to him. Jesus is Lord. If our life could be likened to a boat with an outboard motor, the question is who has control of the rudder? Instead of trying to hold the rudder ourselves, we freely give over control of the rudder to the Lord. This is a gift of trusting faith. From this obedience comes deep intimacy; it is the secret of the true friends of Jesus.

A parable can illustrate this point. A man desires friendship with Jesus. He enthusiastically opens the door of his house to the Lord, and welcomes him to enter. There are many rooms in the man's house.

He is keen to show Jesus around. He takes Jesus into many beautiful rooms, and Jesus is pleased. Then, to the man's dismay, Jesus sees a room he has not been invited to enter. "May I enter this room?", he asks. "Oh, not that room, Jesus!", cries the man as he steers the Lord down another corridor. Because on the door of that room is written "my finances". Then Jesus sees another room, which is barricaded. He asks, "I would love to come into this room." The man replies nervously, "Oh no, not that room, Jesus, there are so many beautiful rooms. You wouldn't want to go to that one." Because over the locked door there is written "my sexuality". In reality the man was only wanting to invite Jesus into the rooms of his life that he felt he had in order. He was keeping the Lord out of those areas which were not in control, and may have been a source of shame and guilt. With mercy and kindness Jesus wants especially to enter the rooms of disorder to bring peace and harmony. If Jesus is not Lord of *all* my life, he is not Lord *at all*.

In the Song of Songs, the bride sings a beautiful song, which can become our song also: "My Beloved is mine and I am his" and "the banner he raises over me is love" (Song 2:16, 4). There are two images suggested here, and both can help us understand what it means to allow Jesus to be our Saviour and Lord. Firstly, it is obviously a nuptial image, which is used often in Scripture to describe the Lord's saving love. The Bridegroom seeks to possess us with his love, and make us his very own. "I will take you for my spouse in righteousness, in steadfast love, and in mercy. I will take you for my spouse in faithfulness; and you shall know the Lord" (Hos 2:19-20). He takes delight in his bride and weds himself to her. "As the bridegroom rejoices over his bride, so shall your God rejoice over you" (Is 62:5). The bride for her part is allowing the Bridegroom to woo her, to persuade her and to "conquer" her with love. So as we open up to the Lord's persuasive love we allow Him to enter our hearts and take us by the heart, to win our hearts with love, and to yield to him totally. He has bound himself to us with unending love. Our "yes" to his love is also unconditional and it binds us to him forever.

The second image in the text is suggested by the raising of the *banner* of love. In the ancient world, when a conquering general took a territory, he had the standard of the King raised over the territory as a sign of victory. When the King of love has been allowed to "conquer" us in the depth of the heart, and has won the territory for himself, then he raises his standard of love within us. The territory has fallen to him; all that was at enmity with Christ has been expelled. All resistance to his Lordship has been defeated. Jesus is Lord. As Paul reminds us, "You are not your own property; you have been bought and paid for" (1Cor 6:19). And the price that was paid to win us from the slavery of sin was very high indeed; not silver or gold, but the precious blood of Jesus (1Pet 1:19). Now we truly belong to the Lord. We freely and joyfully surrender our whole selves, and all that we are, to him in love.

11
Jesus Heals

And wherever Jesus went, into villages or cities or farms, they laid the sick in the marketplaces, and begged him that they might touch even the fringe of his cloak; and all who touched it were healed. Mk 6:56

Jesus is alive! One of the signs of his activity in the Church's life and mission is the manifestation of healing. After they were filled with the Holy Spirit at Pentecost, Peter and John encountered a man begging at the golden gate of the Temple. He had been paralyzed from birth and was well known to everyone. We are told that Peter stared straight at him, and said, "I have no silver or gold, but what I have I give you; in the name of Jesus Christ of Nazareth, stand up and walk" (Acts 3:6). Peter took him by the hand and raised him up. His ankles and feet gained strength, and he went into the Temple "walking and leaping and praising God". By invoking the name of Jesus, Peter called upon the personal presence and power of Jesus. The Risen Christ brought the healing. The early Christians knew from first-hand experience that Jesus of Nazareth was still with them. Jesus is alive! Jesus is Lord!

Jesus, the Messiah – ministry of word and healing

In Luke's gospel Jesus is presented in his earthly ministry as the Messiah. Luke records Jesus' response to John's messengers, who had come to ask him whether he was the Messiah. He had just cured many people of diseases and evil spirits, and had opened the eyes of many blind people. So Jesus replied to them: "Go and tell John what you have seen and heard: the blind receive their sight, the lame walk, the lepers are cleansed, the deaf hear, the dead are raised, the poor have good news brought to them" (Lk 7:22). These were the signs that Isaiah had prophesied would accompany the appearance of the Messiah (Is 61:1-2). Jesus, himself had already identified himself as such, when in the Synagogue at Nazareth he had opened the scroll from Isaiah and declared, "The Spirit of the Lord is upon me, because he has anointed me to bring good news to the poor. He has sent me to proclaim release to the captives and recovery of sight to the blind, to let the oppressed go free, to proclaim the year of the Lord's favor" (Lk 4:18-19).

The public messianic ministry of Jesus had a twofold thrust – a ministry of word, through preaching and teaching, and a ministry of healing and deliverance from evil spirits. Matthew tells us, "Jesus went throughout Galilee, teaching in their synagogues and proclaiming the good news of the kingdom and curing every disease and every sickness among the people" (Mt 4:23). Then the same evangelist tells us that when Jesus sent the Twelve, he gave them a share in this twofold mission of preaching the word and healing. He "gave them authority over unclean spirits, to cast them out, and to cure every disease and every sickness ... As you go proclaim the good news, 'The kingdom of heaven has come near.' Cure the sick, raise the dead, cleanse the lepers, cast out demons ..." (Mt 10:1, 7-8).

In Jesus' ministry of proclaiming the kingdom, healings were integral to the message. They were clear evidence of his divine power; they witnessed to the truth of his words. In the Acts of the Apostles, Peter stresses this point, "Jesus of Nazareth, a man attested to you by God with deeds of power, wonders, and signs that God did through him among you ..." (Acts 2:22). The healings of Jesus were also an expression of his mercy, kindness and tender love. We are told by Mark that a leper came to him, falling to his knees, and begging, "If you want to, you can make me clean." Jesus was "moved with pity." He stretched out his hand and touched the leper. By this surprising action Jesus intended to communicate more than physical healing. By doing so he was declaring an end to the lepers enforced isolation; he was disregarding the laws of ritual purity, and entering into solidarity with lepers to the extent of embracing the possibility of incurring the disease himself. He was motivated by unbounded mercy. He sighed, "Of course, I want to. Be made clean!" (Mk 1:40-41). Immediately the leprosy left the man. Matthew sums up this attitude of compassion throughout the public ministry of Jesus with this report, "When he went ashore, he saw a great crowd; and he had compassion for them and cured their sick" (Mt 14:14).

The Lord's works of healing and deliverance were anticipatory signs of his full work of salvation. They took place at the cost of his bodily sacrifice. Matthew describes the scene at Peter's house in Capernaum, "That evening they brought to him many who were possessed with demons; and he cast out the spirits with a word, and cured all who were sick." Then the gospel writer explicitly links this messianic activity with the suffering borne by the Suffering Servant of Isaiah: "This was to fulfill what had been spoken through the prophet Isaiah, 'He took our infirmities and bore our diseases'" (Mt 8:16-17). This perspective can help us gain a deeper appreciation of the significance that Jesus "touched" the leper. He entered into solidarity with the man's leprous condition. Of course the leprosy was not inflicted on the man because of his personal sin. Nevertheless in a mysterious way all sickness and disease has its origin in the fall of mankind. So the leprosy may be seen as a symbol of the sin that afflicts our soul. Jesus, raised up on the Cross for us, made himself a "leper" for our sake, bearing the disfigurement of our sinful condition, so that we may be healed. Isaiah says, "By his wounds we are healed". All healing flows to us from the wounds of Christ crucified, who is now risen, and his wounds are a font of healing grace for all.

Signs of the Kingdom

The healings of Jesus in the gospel are signs of the in-breaking of the kingdom of God. The power and love of his reign is taking place through his preaching, but also through his healing and deliverance. Pope Benedict XVI declares, "In the miracles of healing performed by the Lord and by the Twelve, God displays his gracious power over the world. They are essentially 'signs' that point to God himself and serve to set man in motion toward God."[56] Their purpose is to witness to the Lord, and to draw the unbeliever into relationship with him. Healing is not an end in itself. The account of the ten lepers suggests that the healing is not complete until the one who is healed is drawn into a relationship with Jesus. The one who is healed should now be ready to acknowledge who Jesus is and worship him (Lk 17:11-19). Like Bartimaeus, the blind beggar, who was healed by Jesus, the healing is meant to lead to discipleship. "Jesus said to him, 'Go; your faith has saved you.' And immediately his sight returned and he followed him along the road" (Mk 10:52).

In some cases Jesus takes the initiative for the healing. An example of this would be the man in the Synagogue with the withered hand, who Jesus ordered to stretch out his hand, and healed him instantly (Mk 3:1-6). And there are other healings of the same kind, such as the woman bent over with an infirmity (Lk 13:10-17) and, the sick man by the pool of Bethzatha, who Jesus says, "Do you want to be healed?" (Jn 5:6). He did not know Jesus, but Jesus healed him anyway. A similar case was the man blind from birth (Jn 9:1-7). However, in most cases people come pleading for healing. These prayers for healing were always welcomed by Jesus. The Roman instruction on prayers for healing says, "The Lord welcomes their requests and the Gospels contain no hint of reproach for these prayers."[57] In these cases it is faith that makes the healing possible, either the faith of the person themselves or the faith of relatives and friends. Before healing the person Jesus often stirred up faith. For example, "Do you believe I can do this?" (Mt 9:28) or "All things are possible to him who believes" (Mk 9:23). On the other hand when he sees people have the faith, he immediately takes action; for example when he saw the faith of the people who lowered down the paralyzed man through the roof (Mt 9:2). After a healing has taken place Jesus often commended the person for his or her faith: to the woman with the hemorrhage he said, "It is your faith that has made you well again" (Mk 5:34).

Healing in the Church

In the Acts of the Apostles, the Church's ministry of preaching and healing in the power of the Spirit continues the ministry of preaching and healing of Jesus of Nazareth. The risen Christ continues to bring his word and healing. After the healing of the paralytic at the Temple Gate, Peter and John were arrested. They testified before the Sanhedrin that "this man is standing before you in good health by the name of Jesus Christ of Nazareth, whom you crucified, whom God raised from the dead ... There is salvation in no one else, for there is no other name under heaven given among mortals by which we can be saved" (Acts 4:9-11). They were acutely aware that the Jesus is Risen, and his saving power was in their midst. Sick people were carried into the street on stretchers so that Peter's shadow may fall on them as he passed. Healing was so readily available. "A great number of people would also gather from the towns around Jerusalem, bringing the sick and those tormented by unclean spirits, *and they were all cured*" (Acts 5:16).

Pope Benedict XVI writes, "Healing is an essential dimension of the apostolic mission and of Christian faith in general."[58] He describes Christianity as a "therapeutic religion". In Latin the word "salus" refers both to salvation and to health. To be saved is to be healed. The deepest wounding of our humanity, as we have seen, is due to our sin. Salvation is ultimately a healing of this wounding of sin, which has alienated us from God, from others, and from ourselves. So the deepest healing is in fact the forgiveness of ours sins, and our restoration to full communion with God, ourselves and others. The Pope says, "Whoever truly wishes to heal man must see him in his wholeness and must know that his ultimate healing can only be God's love."[59]

In the gospels physical ailments are symbolic of the various forms of spiritual infirmity that afflict us in our fallen state – blindness, deafness, or paralysis. Likewise physical healing is an exterior sign of the interior restoration that occurs through forgiveness of sins. The healing of the paralysed man who was lowered through the roof speaks of these two interrelated layers of healing. Jesus first says to the man, "Your sins are forgiven you", going right to the heart of the matter immediately. Then later, to demonstrate the power to forgive sins, he brings the physical healing (Mk 2:1-12). However, it is important to remember that bodily, emotional or spiritual healing (salvation) is never complete until the whole person, body and soul, is taken up in resurrection at the end of time.

Healing through sacraments

The Risen Lord, through the power of the Spirit, continues the work of healing and salvation within the Church and its mission. The sacraments of Christ "touch" us in order to heal us (CC 1504). The Sacrament of Reconciliation ministers the forgiveness of Christ, bringing deep healing. The Sacrament of Anointing heals physical, emotional and spiritual sickness. The Eucharist, in particular, is a source of healing, and has a special power to ensure "bodily health" (CC 1509).

In the gospels, the woman who had suffered from hemorrhages for twelve years, had no doubt endured much pain and humiliation through the crude treatment by physicians, and had no money left from all the medical treatment. She was desperate to reach out to Jesus. Even though there was a crowd bustling around him, she pressed in to touch him. "If I but touch his clothes, I will be made well". Immediately the hemorrhage stopped and she felt in her body she was healed. Of all the people making bodily contact with him, this touch was different. Jesus knew immediately "that power had gone forth from him". He turned around, searching, "Who touched my clothes?" It seemed such a silly question. There were lots of people making contact with his clothes. But this touch of the woman was different. It was a prayer of faith. Power for healing flowed from Jesus because of this faith. He says, "Daughter, your faith has made you well; go in peace, and be healed of your disease" (Mk 5:25-34).

It is like this with the sacraments, and especially the Eucharist. When we come to reach out and "touch" him with faith, healing flows. Before Holy Communion we say the words based on the response of the faith-filled centurion, who has begged Jesus for his servant to be healed: "Lord, I am not worthy for you to enter under my roof, say but the word and my soul shall be healed" (Mt 8:8). We open ourselves to the healing power flowing from the Risen Jesus.

Sr Briege McKenna, who was healed herself of rheumatoid arthritis, has an internationally recognized ministry of healing. She relates an incident when she was attending an outdoor Mass in a mountainous Latin American country.[60] The priest was using an old table for the altar. As Mass was beginning a woman brought a little boy suffering from very severe burns on his body. They prayed with the boy, but Briege admits she was worried because there was no medical help available. The priest said to the woman, "Just leave him under the table here and let's continue with the celebration of the Eucharist". During the Mass Briege was impressed by the faith of the simple, poor people who were celebrating the Mass with such devotion, and she could sense the deep faith of the priest. At the consecration the people were prostrate on the ground, lifting their eyes to Jesus. Briege remembers thinking, "They really believe that this is Jesus." At the end of the Mass she went looking for the little boy. "Where is he?" she asked the mother. "He's over there", she said pointing to the boy, who was running now with the other children. He was completely healed. Briege exclaimed, "But what happened?" The woman simply replied, "What do you mean? Didn't Jesus come?"

Healing ministry today

The Risen Jesus told us that one of the signs that accompany believers is "they will lay their hands on the sick and they will recover"(Mk 16:18). In recent years in the Church, especially inspired by the charismatic renewal, the healing ministry has blossomed in new and fruitful ways. We talk about three dimensions of healing – a) *physical* healing from sickness and bodily disability; b) *psychological* healing of wounds to the human psyche, including emotional wounds. This is sometimes called "inner healing"; and c) *spiritual* healing through the forgiveness of sin, or deliverance from evil spirits. No matter what the focus of our healing ministry we find that these different dimensions overlap and are interrelated. As Dr Philip Madre has insisted, "An authentic charism of healing has to grow through a unified approach to the person: it is always the whole person, in his or her deepest unity, that receives a grace of healing, and not just a part of them, be that physical or psychological or spiritual."[61]

In the "new evangelization" the healing ministry complements the preaching of the word. Inner healing is particularly relevant for the proclamation of the gospel today. The context in which we are proclaiming the gospel has changed dramatically in recent years. We are in an increasingly dysfunctional society, where many people are suffering from the consequences of their own sin or from having been sinned against by others. Relationships have been fractured, and people are suffering inner crises of feeling a sense of worthlessness and lack of purpose. Many are hurting deeply, and are desperate for the Good News of God's love, but don't know whether it exists, or how to find it. We need to preach the redemption by proclaiming the power of Love brought to the world by the Cross of Jesus. When we direct the attention of people towards the wounds of Jesus, we should expect that they will find healing.

A broken heart

Mary, a middle aged woman, had decided to commit suicide. She was deeply depressed and could see no point in living anymore. She had saved up enough pills to make sure it would work. On the chosen day she had closed all the curtains, and sitting in darkness on her lounge was about to end her life. With a twinge of guilt, she prayed, "Lord, forgive me for what I am about to do". Immediately she felt an urge within her to find her Bible. She went off to the bedroom and brought it back, turned on the lamp, and opened it randomly. Her eyes were drawn to the words, "Do not be afraid, I have called you by name, you are mine". It was enough to change her mind. She had seen advertising about a healing Mass to be held in the parish church the next day. She decided to come. After the Mass there was an opportunity to receive prayer for healing, so she went up to the priest for prayer. He asked her, "What would you like me to pray for?" She replied in tears, "A broken heart". As the priest gently laid hands upon her head she felt a warmth come over her, and a new peace enter her heart. Now six months later, smiling, she assures the priest that the peace of Christ has remained with her, the depression has lifted, and she has a new hope and a joy for living.

We seek to meet people in their interior anguish of heart; their loneliness, anxiety, guilt or depression. We need to be able to speak a consoling word in the Spirit and bring the hope of the Risen Christ, but we also need to offer to pray with people, so these deep wounds of the heart can be healed. Prayer for inner healing, when conducted responsibly, brings healing to the wounds of the past, and leads people to greater freedom to be able to live the life of Christian discipleship. In all of this, the gift of forgiveness is a key grace. Usually it is a process which is more or less protracted depending on the depth of the breach of trust that has occurred. We have found that people who experience a new outpouring of the Holy Spirit through the experience of the "baptism in the Spirit" will often find that a new depth of healing will begin to take place in their lives.

Healing in the Spirit

Edwin lost his father through cancer when he was three years old. His eldest brother, Robert, became his natural father-figure. Robert fulfilled the role perfectly, being a good model in faith and character. Edwin loved and revered his older brother as if he was his father. This all changed when Edwin was fourteen. At night time Robert began to sexually molest Edwin, threatening him with severe punishment if he told anyone. "It's alright. It's OK to do this." At first Edwin gave in to his advances out of fear, and also because he was not strong enough to resist. However, one day when Robert had been excessively harsh in beating one of the other children, Edwin in retaliation blurted out the dark secret to their mother. But Robert was so livid at being shamefully exposed and humiliated that he threatened to murder Edwin. For his safety the family arranged for Edwin to live in another house by himself. There was no question about bringing it to the police. Family loyalty prevailed.

Now Edwin was alone, suffering from isolation and rejection. He felt "dirty" because of the abuse, and so felt inclined to do "dirty" things, such as watch pornography and masturbate. He was furious at Robert, and angry at the world. He was angry at God, feeling he had been dealt a raw deal; firstly losing his Father at a young age, and now being abused by his only substitute father figure. He was constantly fearful that his brother would make good his threat to kill him.

After "five months of darkness", one night Edwin heard a soft knock on the door. He opened to find himself facing his older brother. He wanted to slam the door in fear, but before he could do so his brother was asking for forgiveness and embracing him, and begging him to come home. Edwin responded positively, but this was only the beginning of a long process of reconciliation. He wanted to forgive his brother, but it was not easy.

Providentially, a few months after his return to the family home, Edwin attended a Life in the Spirit seminar, where he experienced the "Baptism in the Spirit". When he was prayed over for the Holy Spirit all the memories of the abuse came back to him. Now a deeper healing was taking place. He sensed the Lord assuring him that there was a hidden purpose in all of his suffering: "Even though you gave up on me I did not give up on you. You experienced these terrible things so that you can relate to others and help others in the same plight."

Now a few years later Edwin can honestly say that he loves his brother, and wishes him the best. He knows his brother is not perfect, but he forgives him from the heart. The forgiveness has brought healing. In a recent retreat Edwin had the special grace to recall the only memory he has of his father, which has brought so much joy and freedom to him. He was able to remember when as a three year old boy he was sitting on his father's lap. His father's chin was resting on Edwin's little head, and together they were looking out the front door at the rain coming down. This recollection has brought Edwin much peace. He now has a deeper appreciation of God the Father's love for him.

When charismatic healing is taking place it is a sign of the Kingdom of God taking hold today. It speaks of the once-for-all victory of Jesus in his cross and resurrection, made present here and now. This prayer for healing, in the Catholic Church is best exercised in relationship with the sacraments. The sacraments are the privileged way that

Christ's saving work is made present in the Church. But the healing ministry is not intended to be confined to sacramental ministry alone. We should feel free to pray with others by petition and the laying on of hands at any time that is appropriate. James says, "Why you don't have what you want is because you don't pray for it …" (James 4:2). Jesus says, "I tell you therefore: everything you ask and pray for, believe that you have it already, and it will be yours" (Mk 11:24), and "If you ask for anything in my name, I will do it" (Jn 14:14). Faith in the healing power of Jesus is a fundamental dimension of the saving mission of the Church.

12
Meaning in Suffering

But rejoice in so far as you are sharing Christ's sufferings, so that you may also be glad and shout for joy when his glory is revealed. 1 Pet 4:13

When someone is sick or in emotional anguish the first instinct of the Christian is to pray with the person, and to minister the healing love of God. We exercise our resurrection faith by asking Jesus for healing. Regardless, often people are left unhealed, and must endure their bewildering suffering. Life is never without some measure of pain and suffering. Unexpected calamities are an inevitable part of the human journey – debilitating illness, the premature loss of a loved one, the collapse of one's business – the cross draws near. In the "global village" made so close by modern media we are constantly confronted by natural disasters – bushfires, earthquakes, tsunamis, floods. We could add to this list the senseless savagery of human beings willfully inflicting unjust imprisonment and cruel torture on the innocent, the atrocities of war, the brutality of ethnic cleansing, and so much more evil suffering that afflicts our frail human condition. The cry rises in the human heart, "Why does God allow this to happen?" "Why does he not stop this innocent suffering?" "Where is God?"

Searching for the answer

For centuries the philosophers have been wracking their brains for a solution to the problem of evil, and particularly that of innocent human suffering. There is no logical explanation. But that doesn't mean there is no answer to the question. The answer is only found in faith. Yet, it is not a facile answer, or one that arrogantly dismisses the agony of those who innocently suffer. The answer is found in the paschal mystery of Christ. Anyone who suffers can in a very real way come into contact with the cross of Christ (GS 22). The death and resurrection of Jesus throws new light on suffering, redeems it from within, and enables us to endure it without being totally crushed by it. In fact, suffering united to the cross and resurrection of Jesus can be liberating of the human spirit; a way we experience the power that flows from the wounds of Christ, crucified and risen.

Endeavouring to answer the question of suffering, Raniero Cantalamessa, the preacher to the Papal household, uses a telling image, "What do you do to reassure someone that a particular drink does not contain poison? You drink it yourself first, in front of the other person. This is what God has done for humanity. He has drunk the bitter cup of the Passion. So, human suffering cannot be a poisoned chalice. If God himself has chosen to savor it, the cup of suffering must be more than negativity, loss, absurdity. At the bottom of the chalice, there must be a pearl. We know the name of the pearl: resurrection!"[62] No matter what we suffer in this world it is nothing compared to the glory that is yet to come (Rom 8:18). *The Book of Revelations* gives the promise of ultimate joy, "He will wipe away all tears from their eyes; there will be no more death, and no more mourning or sadness or pain. The world of the past has gone" (Rev 21:4).

Here is one of the deepest meanings of the Cross of Jesus. As Blessed John Paul II said,

> Love is the fullest source of the answer to the question of the meaning of suffering. This answer has been given by God to man in the Cross of Jesus. (SD 13)

Salvific meaning

In the days following the violent attempt on his life, after a long convalescence, Blessed John Paul II wrote an encyclical on the salvific meaning of human suffering. He directs us to the Paschal Mystery. On the cross Christ emptied himself to the ultimate limits of human weakness and impotence – totally identifying himself with the helplessness of suffering. But in and through that very weakness he was lifted up by the power of the Resurrection. The Pope wrote,

> This means that the weaknesses of all human sufferings are capable of being infused with the same power of God manifested in Christ's death and resurrection. (SD 23)

When we suffer we become open and vulnerable to the saving power of God. This is the good news of suffering. Christ has given it new meaning and purpose. Blessed John Paul II goes on to say:

> In him (Christ) God has confirmed his desire to act especially through suffering, which is man's weakness and emptying of self, and he wishes to make his power known precisely in this weakness and emptying of self. (SD 23)

Yet we must be clear that this perspective in no way considers suffering in itself to be good. No, it is an evil in itself. However, we have a God, who on the Cross defeated the power of evil. Out of love for us God has not left us subjugated to evil. He has not abandoned us to suffering in a way that destroys us. God gave his only Son to liberate us from evil. As Pope Benedict XVI says about the Cross, "That which is wrong, the reality of evil, cannot simply be ignored; it cannot just be left to stand. It must be dealt with; must be overcome. Only this counts as true mercy. And the fact that God himself now confronts evil because man was incapable of doing so – therein lies the 'unconditional goodness of God'."[63]

It was God's loving plan to give over his only Son on the Cross "that he may strike at the very roots of human evil and thus draw close in a salvific way to the whole world of suffering in which man shares" (SD 16). Through his solidarity with us Christ entered into the world of human suffering. He knows our suffering from inside, not as a sympathetic observer from outside. He suffered with us in all our temptations, our experiences of misunderstanding and rejection, our fatigue, loneliness and anguish. Jesus deliberately accepted the Father's will for him to be the suffering Messiah. When he began to predict his passion, Peter would have nothing of it. "Lord, this cannot happen to you!" Peter was expecting a glorious messiah figure who would overthrow the Roman yoke of oppression and usher in an era of social and political harmony and prosperity. Jesus, gave his sharpest rebuke to this temptation, "Get behind me Satan; your way of thinking is not God's way but man's" (Mk 8:33). Unless he was to go to his suffering, he would not have been able to redeem suffering from within.

Where is God?

One of the most chilling accounts of human suffering ever written was Elie Wiesel's nobel prize-winning book, *Night*. Wiesel, a deeply religious Jewish boy of fourteen, lost God and his faith in Auschwitz concentration camp in World War II. On the first night at the camp he witnessed children being incinerated in the ovens; watching as their limp bodies were thrown to the flames. The horror was etched into his memory forever. "Never shall I forget those moments which murdered God and my soul and turned my dreams to dust." Even more devastating was the execution of three prisoners suspected of involvement in sabotage of a power station. Eli describes how the prisoners were all assembled to watch. The gallows were erected before them. Three were to be hung, one of them a young boy, "the sad-eyed angel." The three necks were placed with the nooses. The three chairs on which they had been standing were tipped over. Then all the prisoners were forced to walk past the victims as a lesson to all. The two men died quickly. But the boy was too light for his body weight to hang him. As Eli passed by, the boy was still alive, his tongue red, his eyes glazed over, but the rope was still moving due to the struggle. For more than half an hour the boy struggled between life and death, in slow agony before their eyes. A man near Eli was heard to ask, "Where is God now?" Eli sensed a voice within him answer, "Where is he? Here he is – he is hanging here on this gallows."[64]

Wiesel lost his faith in God at that concentration camp. For him God literally hung to death on the gallows, never to be resurrected. His interpretation of the event led him to proclaim the death of God. Yet, the voice in Wiesel actually spoke the truth. God *was* up there with the young boy as he gurgled desperately trying to die. God *was* being hanged with him. This truth is founded in an event that took place almost two thousand years before Auschwitz. God hung on a Cross at Calvary, undergoing the humiliation and agony of Roman crucifixion. God has gone right into the centre of our human suffering. On the Cross he was one with the bewildering suffering of all human beings. He too was innocent, the victim of cruel, senseless torture. In the moment of darkest loneliness and anguish of soul, he cried out, "My God, my God, why have you abandoned me?" The "why?" of every human heart is caught up in that prayer.

On the Cross Jesus received no audible answer to his question. God was silent. But this did not lead him to despair. Rather, he chose to turn his suffering towards the universal good it would produce for all. At that moment of profound self-emptying he was in solidarity with our deepest bewilderment, helplessness and impotence. Absorbing into his human soul all the suffering of the world, he completely trusted the Father, and gave himself over into his loving hands: "Father, into your hands I commend my spirit" (Lk 23:46). Jesus was suffering with that boy on the gallows, just as he suffers with the drug addict shooting up in a Sydney apartment; and with the widow who has lost her husband to cancer; and with the mother who has given birth to a still born child; and with young husband whose wife has abandoned him for another man; and with anyone who is stricken with sickness, grief, rejection, persecution, torture or any of the multitude of human calamities that may come our way.

The deepest pit

Another story from a World War II concentration camp illustrates this point further. At a camp for women at Ravensbrück, Corrie Ten Boom, and her sister Betsie were subject to similar hatred and brutality that Elie Weisel had experienced. They had suffered much cruelty at the hands of the barbarous guards. They were women of deep faith in Christ, but now their faith was being tested to the limit. They were worn down physically by the arduous, long hours working on a rock quarry. The inhumane, debilitating conditions had gotten the better of Betsie, who was dying. As she and Corrie were praying, she had a prophetic insight that Corrie would miraculously survive the camp. Her dying words to Corrie were, "I know you are going to get out of this hell hole. And when you do, I want you to tell the whole world that there is no pit so deep that He is not deeper."[65]

These faith-filled women were in one of the darkest pits of human degradation caused by a brutal and barbaric system. Betsie knew the Cross of Jesus. She knew that Jesus had already gone into the black pit of human cruelty and atrocity when he hung innocently on the Cross as a condemned criminal. Within his soul he experienced the abandonment of human sin, separation from God. He became one with us in our worst extremity of hatred and cruelty to one another. And from that place, the deepest pit of human distress, he put his trust in the Father. Betsie knew that God had entered into the sufferings we inflict on one another and he had redeemed it. She also knew that no matter what we are called to endure in human suffering there will always be hope, because from that place Jesus was raised from the dead.

The agony of Christ continues

When we are in the hour of trial and darkness, when suffering weighs in upon us, we can know in faith the presence of Christ in his agony. Our cries for help to God from deep within our wounded heart are "groans deeper than words" (Rom 8:26). These groans are joined mysteriously, by the Spirit, with the heart of Jesus in the Garden of Gethsemane, as he prayed to the Father. Jesus "offered up prayers and supplications, with loud cries and tears, to the one who was able to save him from death, and he was heard" (Heb 5:7). As St. Leo the Great said, "the Passion is prolonged until the end of time."[66] In the suffering that continues in the world Jesus is present, continuing to suffer with us. As our prayer rises to God, groaning in anguish, he is one with us. Our prayer is his prayer to the Father, who has already lifted him into resurrection, which is our hope as well.

The philosopher Pascal, converted by a profound experience of the fire of God's love, in his famous meditation on the agony of Jesus, says "Christ will be in agony until the end of time".[67] In the Spirit, Jesus is also now in Gethsemane, in the Praetorium, on the way to Calvary, and on the Cross. And this is true mysteriously for the suffering of every person, not only those who are in the Church. We don't claim this to be true "despite" the resurrection; but precisely because of the resurrection. The crucified One is alive and is present with us in our suffering. In the Book of Revelation the victorious Lamb is "standing", meaning he is risen and alive, but also the Lamb is described "as one who was slain", still carrying the signs of immolation and sacrifice (Rev 5:6). There are many hidden Gethsemanes in the world where people undergo interior suffering, sharing in the agony of Jesus. The suffering of Jesus gives consolation and hope. He cried out to the one who could save him, and his prayer was heard. Those who suffer with him are given the assurance that their prayers also will be heeded, and resurrection will be theirs.

A crucifixion parade

At the height of violent pogrom in 2008 that erupted after the death of a revered Hindu Swami in the northern Indian province of Orissa, many Christians were martyred for their faith.[68] Others such as Fr Thomas Chellan and Sr Meena Barwa of the Handmaids of Mary did not lose their lives, but suffered grievously under the persecution. A mob of 500 angry Hindu extremists arrived at the Pastoral Centre at Kandhamal and began to torch the building. Father Thomas and Sr Meena initially escaped and found refuge in the house of some friendly Hindus. However, they were discovered and hauled out of their hiding place. Fr Thomas was doused with kerosene and a man was about to light the match, when someone pushed the assailant away, saving Fr Thomas' life. Sr Meena was stripped and thrown to the ground. One man stepped on her right hand, another on her left, while the third raped her, with others looking on. It was not done out of lust, but was a deliberately diabolical act designed to humiliate her and to violate her vow of chastity, which she had only taken three months earlier. While the rape was happening Fr Thomas tried to stop them, but they beat him all over his body with iron rods. They kicked him, mocked him and ordered him to utter vulgar words, which he refused to do. He had cuts, bruises and swellings all over his body.

After the rape the priest and nun were forced to begin what they later called their "crucifixion parade". The crowd led them still half naked in procession along the street. They were ordering the priest to have sex with Sr Meena, because "that's what priests and nuns do." When he refused, they beat him more. He pleaded for help from the police who were standing nearby, but the police turned away. The beatings with sticks, crowbars, axes and spears continued, as they endured this humiliating Calvary walk of about half a kilometer. Their ordeal only ended when a senior police officer arrived and took control of the situation.

Three years later Sr Meena reflected, "Looking back, I feel that Jesus is not dead on the Cross. He is alive on the Cross and still suffering." She said that she was now grateful to have experienced this crucifixion, "I thank God for choosing me to face this humiliation and giving me the chance to suffer for the people of Kandhamal."[69] She said she had accepted her suffering in the light of faith in Jesus who suffers with us. With the help of others, she has been able to forgive, "I have undergone untold pain in my life. I have met so many people on the way, giving me constant support, love and encouragement. Their presence and care gave me strength to forgive the perpetrators and I am able to reconcile myself with what has taken place."[70]

Fr Thomas says, "Love is sacrifice and to sacrifice for love's sake is a joy which involves suffering. That is the only way. There is no other way besides the cross, and it is there that we will experience true and lasting joy. My trial was Kandhamal, for others it is elsewhere, but only Calvary can transform our human weakness into the fortitude of God … Priests, missionaries or lay people can meet their Calvary anywhere they go. When we respond to the invitation of Jesus to follow in His footsteps and imitate him, we find true life. In our situation, however deplorable it may be, we must accept Calvary and walk along its path. This way, our cross becomes meaningful."[71]

Even though two of the perpetrators received only minor sentences and the others were not brought to justice at all, Fr Thomas says, "I find consolation in the Cross, Christ's forgiveness, and the Virgin's gift of Jesus to humanity. Mary gives us strength to walk in her son's footsteps."

The true Gospel

There is a way of preaching the resurrection of Jesus which is false and misleading. It avoids the mystery of the Cross. The glorious risen Christ still carries his wounds. St Martin de Tours had gone into solitude to seek the Lord and to discover the way of love. While sitting in his cell he was astonished to see a glorious, regal figure appear before him.[72] The figure was dressed in purple imperial robes, with jeweled shoes, and on his head was a golden diadem, with precious stones and pearls. He had a tranquil face, and a benevolent smile, with eyes staring into space suggesting good will to all people.

Martin gazed at the apparition for a long time in silence, seeking to discern whether it was from God, or from his own imagining, or from the devil. At last the glorious figure spoke, "I am Christ, and I am just about to descend to earth, but I wanted to manifest myself to you first." Martin remained silent. The voice spoke again, "Martin why do you hesitate to believe, when you see I am Christ?" Then Martin replied, "I will not believe Christ has come unless he appears as he suffered, showing the marks of his wounds from the Cross." The phantom figure vanished into a puff of smoke.

The Cross is the love of God touching the most painful wounds of our humanity.[73] By his wounds on the Cross Jesus shares in all our loneliness, all our sorrow, all our suffering. The risen Lord still carries these wounds because, having returned to glory, he has not left us from his original descent into our human pain. While in glory he is still suffering with us. The Enemy of our human nature, being consummate hate, cannot replicate the holy wounds of Jesus, which are the proof of the God's love. If the "Christ-figure" is not bearing the wounds it is not authentic. Martin knew this so well because of the circumstances of his conversion. As a young soldier for the Emperor, he was moved with compassion one day when he encountered a beggar, who was almost naked and shivering from cold during a severe frost. Martin cut his own cloak in half with his sword and gave half to the beggar. That night he had a dream in which Christ appeared to him, dressed in that half of the garment which he had given away, saying, "Martin, yet a catechumen, has covered me with his garment."

Strength in weakness

When we gaze upon the wounds of the crucified, Risen Jesus, we find life. In our pilgrim journey here on earth, we will inevitably be wounded through our own actions, and through the actions of others. The Good News is that our wounds do not have to cripple us. Blessed John Paul II reminded us that "The springs of divine power gush forth precisely in the midst of human weakness" (SD 27). This is the meaning of the Cross of Jesus. At his weakest moment, in humiliation and defeat, he became a font of life for the world. All who are willing to enter into this journey with him, by hanging on the Cross with him, will discover a font of life for their own growth and also become a font of life for others.

Though Paul was gifted with mystical favours, he was given a "thorn in the flesh" to stop him from getting proud about these experiences. Even though he pleaded with the Lord about this, he was told, "My grace is enough for you; my power is at its best in weakness" (2 Cor 12:1-9). Paul goes on to say that he will boast only in his weaknesses, "so that the power of Christ may stay over me ... For it is when I am weak then I am strong" (2 Cor 12:10).

There is an important principle here. In and through our wounds, when we unite them with the wounds of Jesus on the Cross, we find a font of grace within ourselves, and we can become a font of grace for others. Rather than be afraid of our wounds, we can bring our wounded heart to the Lord of all mercy and allow healing to flow to us from his sacred wounds. This does not mean that our wounds disappear. To desire this would be to want to go beyond Christ himself, who still carries his wounds in his Risen Body. However, by the healing power of his wounds we are delivered from any negative impact that our wounds may have upon us; and by the miracle of his redeeming love our wounds can become the very source of our apostolic life and service of others.

13
Amazing Love

So we have known and believe the love that God has for us.
1 Jn 4:16

Down through the centuries men and women have been deeply touched by the redeeming love of God in Jesus Christ. Paul, the apostle, was a great witness. He prays in Ephesians "that Christ may dwell in your hearts by faith"; and that "you would come to know the breadth and length and height and depth" of the love of Christ (Eph 3:17-19). This amazing love of Christ is most visible through the eyes of faith when we look upon the Cross of Jesus. Gazing upon the Cross, we can see the *height* of his love symbolized by the vertical beam reaching upwards. As the psalmist says, "his love reaches to the heavens." He has opened heaven's door for us, reconciled us with God, and won for us a "crown of righteousness" that awaits us, when we finally come to him in glory.

With our eyes still fixed on the Cross we can see the *depth* of Christ's love, symbolized by the beam planted deep in the earth. Jesus loved us so much that he did not cling to his equality with God, but emptied himself, becoming one of us, born in a stable, and placed as an infant in a feeding trough for animals. His love went deeper still, emptying himself further, being crucified by the Romans as a common criminal. Lower than this it would seem he could not have gone. But then he emptied himself further by giving himself to us in the Eucharist under the appearance of bread and wine.

Now if we turn our gaze to the horizontal beam of the Cross, we can feel in our hearts the *breadth* of his love. With his arms outstretched on this beam, he embraced every human being. With his Mother, and John the Beloved disciple, at the foot of the Cross, he entrusted every disciple to his Blessed Mother and gave her to each one of us. But his love goes beyond the inner circle of his beloved disciples. His saving love is universal in its reach. No one is excluded. His heart is big enough to offer a place for all men and women in the Father's house. There are no distinctions of gender, race, colour or creed. No matter whether wealthy or poor, sick or healthy, famous or unknown, success or a failure, he died for all. He came to seek out and save the lost; his heart on the Cross embraces the drug dealers, the prostitutes, the serial murderers, the rapists, the porn pushers, the pedophiles – he died for all.

As we look upon the Cross we will also discover the meaning of the *length* of his love. His love has *infinite* duration. It endures until the end of time; and beyond time *forever*. His love is everlasting. It has no end! He will never stop loving us, even if we reject him. He has irrevocably bound himself to us in love when he was nailed to the Cross for our sake. The covenant, which he will never break, was written in his blood, and carved on his hands and his feet and his side, forever. Now Risen, he still carries his wounds as a sign of his eternal love for us.

The Divine Bridegroom

When we say "yes" to the love of Jesus, lifted up on the Cross for our sins, and raised by the Father for our deliverance, he fills us with this love. Bernard of Clairvaux struggled to describe this experience, which is by definition indescribable:

> When the Bridegroom, Christ the Word, came to me he never made any sign that he was coming; there was no sound of his voice, no glimpse of his face, no footfall. He made no movement by which I could identify his coming; none of my senses showed me that he

had flooded the depths of my being. Only by the warmth of my heart did I know that he was there. I knew the power of his might because my guilt and sin were wiped away and my body's yearnings were brought under control … To those who have experienced this, I say: Relish it. To those of you who have not, I say: Burn with desire, that you might come to experience it.[74]

From the ugliness of sin to the beauty of God

St Augustine encountered this love. He says, "You loved me when I was unlovable, and because you loved me you made me lovable". However, it was only after a long journey of heartfelt searching that he finally yielded to God's love. As a young man he tried on the various ideologies of his day.[75] But they all failed him. He also was captive to "the bonds of illicit love." But this did not satisfy his deepest desire. By God's providence he came under the preaching of Ambrose, the bishop of Milan, and was convicted by the truth of the word of God. But knowing the truth, he was still in bondage to the flesh. He found himself in bitter torment; knowing what he should do, but incapable of doing it. "I twisted and turned in my chain … In my heart I kept saying, 'let it be now, let it be now!'" He was on the point of resolution, but he could not do it. Weeping he cried out, "How long shall I go on saying 'tomorrow', 'tomorrow'? Why not now? Why not make an end of ugly sins at this moment?" Then he heard the voice of a child singing: "Take and read; take and read!" Augustine took this as the voice of the Lord calling him to pick up the Bible that was nearby. It fell open to the words, "Let us cast off the armour of darkness and put on the armour of light … Put on the Lord Jesus Christ, and make no provision for the flesh, to gratify its desires" (Rom 13:13-14).

In that instant Augustine received from God the grace of conversion in his soul. He said, "the light of confidence flooded into my heart and all the darkness of doubt was dispelled." He was 33 years old, and now after a long search he had found the Lord. Rather, the Lord had found him. In his Confessions, written in praise of God's love, he recalls the grace of conversion this way:

> Late have I loved you, O Beauty so ancient and so new; late have I loved you! For behold you were within me, and I outside; and I sought you outside, and in my ugliness fell upon those lovely things that you have made. You were with me and I was not with you ... You called and cried to me and broke open my deafness; and you sent forth your beams and shone upon me and chased away my blindness: you breathed fragrance upon me, and I drew in my breath, and do now pant for you: I tasted you, and now hunger and thirst for you: you touched me, and I have burned for your peace.[76]

From knowing to loving

There is a profound difference between knowing about Christ and *knowing* Christ. The first comes from acquired knowledge, the second from experience. Many scholars have studied the mysteries of the faith, and written profound treatises on what has been revealed in Jesus Christ. But at some point or other in everyone's journey, the Lord Jesus turns to the individual and looks into his or her eyes, asking the question he asked of his first disciples, "Who do you say I am?" Thomas Aquinas was one of the greatest theologians of the mediaeval times. He brilliantly synthesized the mysteries of faith, using the underpinning of newly found Aristotelian philosophy. We still rely upon his synthesis today. But his work was left unfinished. Towards the end of his life as he was praying before the Blessed Sacrament, he had a moment of mystical revelation of the Risen Christ. He did not write again. His secretary asked him why he stopped writing. Thomas replied, "All that I have written seems to me like so much straw compared to what I have seen and what has been revealed to me." Thomas had been taken more deeply than ever into the mystery of "the love of Christ which surpasses all knowledge" (Eph 3:19).

From being lukewarm to a heart on fire

Teresa of Avila came to know the fire of God's love within her soul like few others. But it had not always been so. She had for twenty years been trying to live a committed spiritual life. But she found the practice of prayer a tiresome chore. She had made little compromises in her life; her heart was divided between its allegiance to Christ and its attraction to worldly pleasures. Then one day, out of the blue, she received the gift of a "second conversion."[77] She was filled in a new way by the love of God. It happened like this. She was walking into the chapel one evening, as she had done for years. Her eyes fell on an image of "a very wounded Christ." It was a picture of Jesus suffering in his passion. She had not seen it before. It struck her to the core. As she gazed upon this image, she had a new insight into what Jesus had undergone when he suffered for us. She says, "I felt how poorly I had thanked him for those wounds; I thought my heart was breaking, and I threw myself before Him while shedding many tears, begging him to give me the grace never to offend him again." This was a profound turning point in her journey, a moment of repentance before the Cross, realizing how much her sins had crucified the Lord, and receiving a new infusion of love for him as our Saviour. The fire of God's love at that moment seared into her soul propelling her forward in her spiritual journey.

Saved by grace

It does not matter whether we are sunken in the mire of sin, or a "card-carrying" follower of Christ, when we come before the Cross of Jesus in the light of God's revelation our hearts can be opened again. We can have new eyes to see the truth of our broken, sinful state; and to humbly acknowledge that our only hope is our Redeemer. John Newton was an 18th century slave-trader. Even though raised as a Christian, he had renounced any need for religion. He crossed the ocean several times as a coarse, cruel captain of a slave ship.

The awful degradation of the slaves in the galley of his ship was no concern to him.

Then, during a terrible storm, which almost wrecked his ship, and killed many of its human cargo, Newton cried out to God for mercy. This was the beginning of his conversion. He later became a minister in the Church of England, and joined William Wilberforce in the fight against slavery. Newton never lost sight of the saving grace which he had received; the grace that turned his life around. In 1779 he wrote the legendary song "Amazing Grace", which rose out of his heart now converted to the Lord. When he wrote "saved a wretch like me", he really meant the words with all his heart. He knew that God had taken him from a bondage more wretched than that of the slaves he had carried on his ship. God in Christ had won him from slavery to freedom, from death to life.

In this book I have sought to sing the same song, but with an altered title, *Amazing Love*. It's a song of gratitude to our Saviour, who has rescued us from sin, and given us new life. It's a song of hope in the victory of Christ who has burst out of the tomb, broken our chains, and set us free. It's a song of joy for our Beloved who has redeemed us by the shedding of his blood and made us his very own. It's a song of praise to God whose amazing love revealed in the crucified and risen Christ is everlasting.

Postscript

THEOLOGY OF REDEMPTION

Ultimately the mystery of Redemption transcends intellectual analysis. We are invited by the Spirit to enter into it by faith. Nevertheless, faith seeks understanding. Theologians have developed various theories to explain what we have experienced in the Redemption, which was won for us by Jesus Christ through his death and resurrection. In the history of redemption theory there have been three major models that have provided us with a way of trying to explaining the mystery. These models offer three perspectives by which we can in some way penetrate the mystery. Preachers of the redemption often favour one of these models over the others, and draw their images from that perspective. Each approach is substantiated by Scripture, and preachers will favour the Scripture texts which fit with their own perspective. However, no one model by itself is sufficient to explain the mystery. Each model is necessary, and they complement one another. The challenge for theologians and preachers is to find an integration of all three approaches.

In his classic work, *Christus Victor*,[78] Gustaf Aulen teased out these three models of Redemption which have served the Church in articulating the mystery.

a) Redemption as liberation

This approach was the favourite of the early Greek Fathers, especially St Ireneaus. It has the strength of uniting the death and resurrection of Jesus in one single movement. The emphasis is on the victory won by Jesus in defeating the powers of darkness that previously kept mankind captive. Enslaved to sin and subjected to demonic forces, humanity needed to be liberated. The death of Jesus on the Cross broke the power of Satan, and his resurrection and ascension put all powers of evil under his feet. In this book the *Liberation Theory* is found articulated mainly in Chapter 8.

Some commentators claim that this approach doesn't include our decision-making as such. We are left as spectators of a cosmic battle happening "out there" which is won by Christ, but does not involve us. In Chapter 8 I addressed this criticism by emphasizing our "yes" to what has been applied to our lives through our immersion into the victorious death and resurrection of Jesus in Baptism.

Other contemporary commentators tend to dismiss this theory because they consider the cosmic battle with the powers of evil to be mythological or medieval nonsense. This view fails to be true to the Scriptural revelation and the teaching of the Church.

b) **Redemption as expiation**

The classic presentation of this approach was given by Anselm of Canterbury (+1098) in his work *Cur Deus Homo?* It was called the *Satisfaction Theory*. The term "satisfaction" has its roots in the traditional penitential practice, which insists that even after we have been forgiven our sins we need to make "satisfaction" for them. This term from penitential practice was taken by Cyprian and applied by analogy to Christ's atonement. Christ's sacrifice was a compensatory "satisfaction" made to God for us.

The theory sees humanity's sin as dishonouring God. The offence is measured by the dignity of the one offended. God's honour is infinite; so mankind's guilt is infinite. This is not a personal offence against God; he cannot be offended in this way. We cannot take away from his splendor, glory and honour. If humanity no longer acknowledges God, it does nothing to his intrinsic honour and glory, but it affects the whole order of relationships in the universe. After sin it is not God's personal honour that has to be restored, but the disfigurement of the world. Because of sin the world is out of joint. It remains in order only in so far as it upholds the honour of God. The whole intelligible order has been disrupted and dislocated by sin. Mankind was created for obedience, and service of God. So sin has thwarted this purpose.

Reparation needed to be made by humanity. This called for an infinite satisfaction made to God. But we are finite human beings. We could not make the restitution that was necessary. We were incapable of doing it. Only God could do it. But it had to be a human being who makes the infinite recompense to God in payment for the offence against his justice and trust in us. There was no son of Adam to fulfill this role. One man had to offer a perfect sacrifice of obedience to the Father on behalf of all. This man could not be found on the face of the earth. This is why God became man. There had to be a human being who could make the act of infinite satisfaction for us. This had to be a God-man.

In this book I have deliberately avoided using the term "satisfaction," since in modern parlance it is difficult to explain. It runs the risk of giving the impression that redemption was about what we had to do towards God, rather than what God has done for us. However, I have sought to present an approach to redemption as expiation which sufficiently addresses the issues pertinent to Anslem's theory. In chapters 3 and 4 I have used the concept of "solidarity"; in chapter 4 I have focused on the concept of "substitution" and in chapter 6 I have used the concept of "sacrifice". All of these concepts are necessary for an adequate expression of the objective redemption; explaining how God has overcome the unbridgeable gap between humanity and the divinity caused by sin. The strength of this expiation model is that it seeks to show *how* we were redeemed. It is concerned with the death of Jesus as the efficient cause of the atonement.

While I have developed a "substitution" theory, using Hans Urs Von Balthasar, I have tried to avoid any hint of a *"penal* substitution theory". In chapter 6 I seek to make clear the primary problem of the penal approach, which developed as a distortion of Anselm's theory. Any notion that Jesus took our place in order to placate the anger of God needs to be repudiated, since it presents a false idea of God. On the other hand, while stressing the mercy of God, I have not overlooked his justice. The concept of the "wrath of God" which I explain as an objective reality due to our sin, suggests that sin has consequences of just punishment. But it is a punishment that we bring upon ourselves, not a punishment which is meted out upon us by an angry and vengeful God. In all theories of redemption we must keep uppermost in our minds that God is Love, and that truth never changes.

c) Redemption as transforming love

This approach emerged in the tradition as a reaction to Anselm's theory, which seemed to be preoccupied with the objective redemption and not sufficiently attentive to the subjective transformation in the individual through appropriation of Christ's atoning work. Rather than be concerned about the efficient causality of the death of Jesus, it emphasized the exemplary causality of Jesus' passion and death. The champion of this approach was Peter Aberlard (1079-1142).

Jesus on the Cross is a compelling witness of love. His salvific work is accomplished through his overwhelming, persuasive, and infectious love which transforms hearts. So the human person dwelling upon the passion and death of Jesus is overcome and motivated by his saving love. The emphasis is on God's supreme initiative of love. The Cross is a gratuitous gift of grace drawing us irresistibly back into relationship with God.

In this book, chapter 5 focuses on the Transforming Love approach. I have intentionally changed the order in which the three models appeared in history, attempting to use this model as the one that integrates the whole work of the redemption, since it is founded on God's love. The reason why God became a man, why Jesus went to the Cross, and why the Father raised him from the dead is Love. It is my conviction that Redemption theology should proclaim the motive of God's love first and be informed by God's love throughout.

This approach draws upon the classic Scripture texts: "The proof that God loves us is that Christ died for us while we were still sinners" (Rom 5:6-8). "The Good Shepherd is the one who lays down his life for his sheep" (Jn 10:11). "No greater love has any man than he lay down his life for his friends" (Jn 15:13). "This is the love I mean; not our love for God, but Gods love for us, when he sent his Son to be the sacrifice that takes our sins away" (1 Jn 4:10).

For this model to be complete it needs the expiatory model. Of itself it does not explain well the "how" of the redemption. However, it is worth noting that the transforming power of God's love is much more than the example of Jesus on the Cross, which might be looked upon in a detached way from a distance. Rather, the love of Christ has inherent power to change us and recreate us. This model is also helped by the *Liberation Model*, which further explains the victory that had to be accomplished for us by Christ's death and resurrection

This model helps us to know the love of God in the heart of Jesus in his passion and death. Through revelation from the Holy Spirit, as we look upon the One whom we have pierced, our hearts are pierced with the truth of what God has done for us (Jn 19:37). By dwelling upon Jesus Crucified, whose side was pierced by the lance for our sake, from which flowed blood and water for the salvation and sanctification of all, our hearts are opened. This revelation is the starting point and the centre-piece of an understanding of the mystery of the redemption. For this reason I have tried to use this third model to draw together all the other perspectives around the one central affirmation of God's saving love for us in Jesus crucified and risen.

ENDNOTES

1. The late Cardinal Avery Dulles, renowned U.S. ecclesiologist, said in a talk at Fordham University in 1992, "In my judgment the evangelical turn in the ecclesial vision of Popes Paul VI and John Paul II is one of the most surprising and important developments in the Catholic Church since Vatican II ... For them the heart and centre of evangelization is the proclamation of God's saving love as shown forth in Jesus Christ. Where the name of Jesus is not spoken, there can be no evangelization in the true sense ...", Avery Dulles, *John Paul II and the New Evangelization* (N.Y.: Fordham University, 1992) p. 3.

2. These characteristics of the "new evangelization" were given in a talk to Latin American bishops. See John Paul II, "The Task of the Latin American Bishops," *Origins*, 12 (March 24, 1983): 659-62.

3. Pope John Paul II, *Ad Limina* visit of Bishops of Southern Germany, December 4, 1992, *LÓsservatore Romano* (English ed.), March 14, 1988, p. 5.

4. Raniero Cantalamessa, *First Advent Sermon*, Part 2, given to Pontifical household, Dec. 2, 2005, in *Zenit News*, the World seen from Rome, Friday 23rd December.

5. Pope John Paul II, *LÓsservatore Romano*, (English Edition), March 24, 1993, p.3.

6. Pope Benedict XVI, Christmas Address to Roman Curia, Dec. 22, 2011 in *Zenit News*, The World seen from Rome, December 22, 2011.

7. St. Bonaventure, *In II Sent.* 1, 2, 2, 1. Quoted in CC 293.

8. St Thomas Aquinas, *Sent.* 2, Prol., Quoted in CC 293.

9. St Irenaeus, *Adv. Haeres*, 4, 20, 7.

10. Quoted in Raniero Canatalamessa, *Life in the Lordship of Christ*, (Kansas City: Sheed and Ward, 1989) p. 13.

11. See exposition of this in Gerald O'Collins SJ, *Jesus Our Redeemer*, (Oxford: University Press, 2007) pp. 29-32.

12. For example, Maximus the Confessor, "This is the great and hidden mystery ... This is the divine purpose foreknown prior to the beginning of created things". (*Ad Thalassium*, 60).

13. St Augustine, *Contra Faustum*, 22. 27 This and following quotes from Augustine taken from Gerald O'Collins, *Jesus our Redeemer*, op. cit. pp. 56-57.

14. St Augustine, *De Civitate Dei*, 14. 13.

15. St Augustine, *De Libero Arbitrio*, 2. 53.

16. This is a phrase used by C.S. Lewis, quoted in Leanne Payne, *The Broken Image: Restoring Personal Wholeness through Healing*, (Grand Rapids: Baker publishing, 1995), p. 125.

17. Maximus the Confessor, quoted in CC 400.

18. Cardinal John Henry Newman, *The Dream of Gerontius*, 1865, in hymn "Praise to the Holiest in the Height".

19. Catherine of Siena, *The Dialogue*, trans. Suzanne Noffke, O.P. (London: SPCK,1980), p. 49, p. 325.

20. Pope Benedict XVI, *Jesus of Nazareth* Part II (San Francisco: Ignatius, 2011) p. 155.

21. Ibid., p. 163.

22. John Saward, *The Mysteries of March: Hans Urs Von Balthasar on the Incarnation and Easter* (London: Harper Collins, 1990), p. 43.

23. Ibid.

24. Story comes from Jack Canfield and Mark Victor Hansen, *Chicken Soup for the Soul* (Florida: health Communications, 1993) pp. 27-28.

25. Reported on www.npr.org – Kelly Kennedy, March 2010. Also www.youtube. com/watch, 23 May 2008 – Medal of Hounour – Pte. Ross McGinnis; Staff Sgt. Ian Newland.

26. Rev. Antonio Ricciardi, *St. Maximilian Kolbe* (Boston: St Paul Editions, 1982) also Boniface Hanley, *No Greater Love* (Notre Dame Indiana: Ave Maria Press, 1982).

27. Pope Paul VI, *Homily*, Beatification of Maximilian Kolbe, Oct 17, 1971.

28. Pope John Paul II, *Homily*, Canonisation of Maximilian Kolbe, Oct 10, 1982

29. Boniface Hanley, op. cit., pp. 75-76 .

30. Thomas Aquinas, *Summa Theologica* III, p. 47, a.3.

31. Papal letter on 50th Anniversary of 'Haurietis Aquas,' accessed from *Zenit News* on 11/20/2007.A.A.S.98 (2006) c.f. *Deus Caritas Est*, 7.

32. Joseph Cardinal Ratzinger, *Behold the Pierced One: An approach to a Spiritual Christology*, trans. Graham Harrison (San Francisco: Ignatius Press, 1986), p. 64.

33. Blaise Pascal, *Pensees* (1669), 1.1.4, 277.

34. See Ken Barker, *His Name is Mercy* (Melbourne: Modotti Press, 2010) passim

35. The story is told in Phillip Yancey, *What Good is God?* (London: Hodder & Stoughton, 2010) pp. 264-265.

36. Mother Teresa, *Come be my Light*, ed. Brian Kolodiejchuk, M.C., (N.Y.: Doubleday, 2007) p. 155.

37. Ibid., p. 325.

38. Ibid., p. 157.

39. Ibid., p. 159.

40. A good critique of this theory is found in Gerald O'Collins, *Jesus Our Redeemer* (UK: Oxford University Press, 2007) pp. 133-16.

41. See Raniero Cantalamessa, *Life in the Lordship of Christ*, op.cit., pp. 107-109

42. Grant Macdonald, *A Father's Promise*, 1997, at www.grantsgraceland.org.

43. This reflection draws upon the catechesis of Pope John Paul II, "Behold Your Mother!" General Audience, November 23, 1988.

44. Thomas Aquinas, *Summa Theologica*, 3a.48.3 resp.

45. A good summary of the issues around the concept of "sacrifice" in relation to the redemption can be found in Gerald O'Collins, *Jesus our Redeemer*, op. cit., pp. 162-172.

46. For this section I am indebted to Pope Benedict XVI, *Jesus of Nazareth*, Part II, op. cit., pp. 39-40, 231-235.

47. *Romero*, A Paulist Pictures Production of a John Duigan Film. Starring Raul Julia (Four Seasons Entertainment Inc.: 1989).

48. Given in Sheila Cassidy, *Good Friday People* (London: Darton, Longman and Todd, 1991) p. 130.

49. Joseph N. Tylenda, *Jesuit Saints and Martyrs*, 2nd ed. (Chicago: Loyola Press, 1998) pp. 136-138.

50. Augustine, Enarr, Ps. 120, 6; CC 40, p. 1791. Quoted in Raniero Cantalamessa, *Life in the Lordship of Christ*, op. cit., p.79.

51. St Augustine, *Sermo Denis*, 7 (Miscellanea Agostiniana, 1, p. 32), quoted Raniero Cantalamessa, *The Mystery of Easter* (Collegeville, Minesota: The Liturgical Press, 1993), p. 37.

52. Pope Paul VI, Wednesday Audience, *L'Osservatore Romano*, November 23, 1972.

53. John Paul II, Wednesday Audience, 1983.

54. The need to "make satisfaction for our sins" comes after the gift of justification has been freely given, and even then, when making satisfaction, we can do nothing by ourselves. We can only do what is necessary by the grace of Christ who strengthens us. In this regard, the *Catholic Catechism* quotes an illuminating passage from the Council of Trent (CC 1460).

55. The doctrine of "merit" is founded on the sovereignty of grace. "The saints have always had a lively awareness that their merits are pure grace." (CC 2011) We can only merit anything for our salvation and sanctification as a result of receiving the Holy Spirit and grace first. (CC 2010).

56. Pope Benedict XVI, *Jesus of Nazareth*, Part I, (N.Y.: Doubleday, 2007), p. 177

57. Congregation for the Doctrine of the Faith, *Instruction on Prayers for Healing*, I, 2, in Prayer for Healing, International Colloquium Rome, 2001, (Rome: ICCRS, 2003) p. 310.

58. Pope Benedict XVI, ibid., p. 176.

59. Ibid., p. 176.

60. Briege McKenna, O.S.C., *Miracles do Happen* (London: Pan Books/Veritas publications, 1987) pp. 59-60.

61. Dr. Philippe Madre, "Psychology of Healing", Congregation for the Doctrine and Faith, *Instruction on Prayer for Healing*, p. 231.

62. Raniero Cantalamessa, *Good Friday Homily*, April 22, 2011, on *Zenit News*.

63. Pope Benedict, *Jesus of Nazareth*, Part II, p.123.

64. Elie Wiesel, *Night* (N.Y.: Avon Books, 1969) pp. 75-76.

65. Corrie Ten Boom, *The Hiding Place* (London: Hodder and Stoughton, 1971)p. 195 The words given here are taken from a motion picture, *The Hiding Place*, and written in inset of pictures in the book between p. 112 and p. 113.

66. St. Leo the Great, *Sermo*, 70, 5: PL 54, 383.

67. B. Pascal, *Pensees*, n. 553.

68. Anto Akkara, *Shining Faith in Kandhamal* (Bangalore: Asian Trading Cooporation, 2009) pp. 59-68.

69. Ibid. pp. 63, 65.

70. Meena Barwa, Orissa: *Raped nun forgives aggressors and recounts her suffering*, www.asianews.it, 12/7/2011.

71. Nirmala Carvalho, *Christ's love overcomes Calvary, even here in Orissa*, www.asianews.it, 4/1/2010.

72. Christopher Donalson, *Martin of Tours: Parish Priest, Mystic and Exorcist* (London: Routledge & Kegan Paul, 1980) p. 93.

73. Pope John Paul II, *Dives in Misericordia*, n. 8.

74. Killian Walsh and Irene Edmonds, *Bernard of Clairveaux's Writings*, Kalamazo: Cistercian Publications).

75. St Augustine, *Confessions* (London: Penguin Books, 1961) pp. 21-179

76. Ibid. Bk 7, 10, 27.

77. Teresa of Avila, *Life*, Chapters 7-8.

78. Gustaf Aulen, *Christus Victor* (Oregon: Wipf and Stock Publishers, 2003; previously SPCK, 1931).

Fr Ken Barker is the founder of the Missionaries of God's Love (MGL), a new emerging congregation in the Australian Church. He is involved in many works of evangelisation and spiritual renewal, including Disciples of Jesus Community, charismatic renewal and the Young Men of God Movement.

Previous books by the author:

> *Becoming Fire*
> *A Radical Way of Love*
> *Young Men Rise Up (Connor Court)*
> *His Name is Mercy (Modotti Press)*
> *A Light for my Path*

www.ingramcontent.com/pod-product-compliance
Lightning Source LLC
Chambersburg PA
CBHW060157190426
43199CB00044B/2642